Power and Choice

Power and Choice

The Formulation of American Population Policy

Peter Bachrach
Temple University
Department of Political Science

and

Elihu Bergman
Harvard University
Center for Population Studies

Lexington Books
D.C. Heath and Company
Lexington, Massachusetts
Toronto   London

Library of Congress Cataloging in Publication Data

Bachrach, Peter
  Power and choice.

    1. United States—Population, I. Bergman,
Elihu, joint author.   II. Title.
HB3505.B29   301.32'9'73   72-3545
ISBN 0-669-84293-1

Published simultaneously in Canada.

Printed in the United States of America.

International Standard Book Number: 0-669-84293-1

Library of Congress Catalog Card Number: 72-3545

To Our Women of Valor
Florence Bachrach and
Liz Bergman

Contents

List of Figures

Acknowledgments

For critical reading of all or part of the manuscript and for friendly encouragement, we wish to express our gratitude to A.E. Keir Nash, University of California at Santa Barbara; and Allan P. Sindler, University of California at Berkeley; Roger Cobb and Charles Elder, University of Pennsylvania; Moye Freymann and William Flash, University of North Carolina; Abraham David, Research Triangle Institute; Thomas Lyons, Agency for International Development; and Roger Revelle, Harvard University.

Our decision to collaborate in writing this book stems from our participation in the First Workshop on Political Science in Population Studies sponsored by the Carolina Population Center in December 1970.

The exploration of population policy formulation processes has been moved forward by the International Population Policy Consortium. Our association with the Consortium has provided added incentive for our work and we are grateful for the keen interest of our Consortium colleagues in the U.S. and abroad.

We owe a special debt to Joy March, Mary Ellen Urann, Larry Weeks, Monica Schisler and Robert Klugman for their many services as secretaries, political researchers and proof readers.

Power and Choice

1

A Power Approach to Policy Formulation

Power and Policy-Making

This book is about power and choice, specifically how power is employed in expanding or limiting choices in a process of policy formulation.

To focus the inquiry we have selected a policy area which is relatively new and in which the stakes are not yet fully determined. This is the area of population policy-making. Aside from its newness, we consider this area both intriguing and important because it involves a concern with the behavior and life-style of large groups of people and the objective of increasing their opportunities for well-being.[1]

For a concept of power, we have sought a comprehensive interpretation which is most suitable for application to the process of policymaking. The generally accepted definition of power by political scientists states that "A has power over B to the extent that he can get B to do something that B would not otherwise do."[2] For our purposes, this definition is unsatisfactory for two reasons: First, the definition clearly infers that a power relationship requires A consciously to exercise sanctions over B, and B to comply to A's wishes. If either of these decisions by A and B is not forthcoming, it cannot be said that power has been exercised. Thus if A is unaware of the existence of B, or of the fact that B has altered his own behavior in accordance with his anticipation of what he believes to be the wishes of A, a power relationship does not exist. Within a macro framework of analysis, this is a serious limitation of the definition. For in reality it is a common experience that A is oblivious of B's anticipated reaction to him.

Second, the definition also is not useful in a macro context when the relationship between A and B is an indirect one. As we have seen, in a direct relationship between two agents, power cannot be said to have been exercised if B refuses to comply to A's wishes. Consider, however, the case where A gets what he wants in spite of defiant action by B. For example, it often is more effective to undermine the credibility or legitimacy of the opposition than to attempt to silence him by a direct threat of sanctions. He continues to pound his fist and speak, but to no avail. No one listens. He is rendered isolated or ineffectual in face of the attitudes or actions of other actors who have been influenced by A. To claim that power has not been exercised in this case—on the ground that B did not comply to A's demands—is to ignore one of the most effective routes that a power wielder may choose to control dissident individuals and groups.

To avoid both of these major defects in our analysis, we must adopt a macro-oriented conception of power. We thus define power as the utilization of resources, ranging from skills, money, and legitimacy, to charisma and instrumentalities of violence, which have the direct or indirect effect of modifying the behavior of other actors in accordance with the preferences of the power wielder.[3]

In focusing upon how public policy is shaped and by whom, the political analyst also has traditionally assumed that political power is most clearly reflected in the disposition of issues. He has consequently centered his attention on the decision-making arena, the process of making choices about issues, and upon other factors such as the related background, commitments, and ideologies of participants in the decision-making process, on their resources of power, including support from other political actors, and, most importantly, on whether the visible policy proposals—preferably "key" proposals—are adopted or rejected. Thus for all practical purposes the powerful are decision-makers whose policy preferences most often prevail in the course of political combat.[4]

This approach to policy analysis is fundamentally defective since it fails to take into account major obstacles to the conversion of not-so-visible wants and preferences into policy issues and choices. It overlooks the possibility that power may be exercised to prevent the transformation of demands into issues, and to keep certain public wants invisible. By utilizing power in this way, demands can be submerged, subdued, or side-tracked so that they are not introduced into the decision-making arena.

Perhaps a classic example of this phenomenon is the treatment accorded to wants of the American black community prior to the civil rights revolution in the 1960s. Here was an entire cluster of wants and demands that remained covert because of the actions and inactions that prevented them from becoming overt political issues. Thus can power be exercised in a way which is not manifest within the actual decision-making arena. More importantly, political power may be exercised where overt political demands or issues are not present. Indeed, one of the most effective uses of power is to prevent the emergence of articulated demands and their translation into issues; and, thus, to suppress overt political conflict.[5]

Even when wants and demands become articulated in a recognizable form, they can be suppressed or aborted before their effective entry into the decision-making apparatus of the political system. Here again, power is exercised to deny them this entry. Once more citing the experience of the American black community, their demand for effective exercise of the franchise, though recognized for many years, was prevented from being considered on its merits within the decision-making arena because of endless series of filibusters in the Senate. The exercise of power by a small group of Senators averted a decision on the relevant legislation. Thus power was used to abort the decision-making process when the demands had succeeded in surfacing and the issues were clear.

The use of power in limiting choice-making, thus suppressing conflict, is the key to our analysis of population policy-making in the United States. We are interested in how the principal actors within this particular policy-making apparatus have been able to control the policy agenda to favor their preferences in the face of significant opposing positions.

We will speculate on how the nature of this policy-making apparatus equips its principal participants with the capability to limit the range of conflict and choice. Within this context, we will consider the linkage between two means of exercising power in policy-making: (a) the power to shape and define the policy issue—primarily the scope and nature of the problem and the goals sought—within the arena where policy is formulated and (b) the power to prevent hostile proposals or approaches from being seriously considered within this same arena.

There are a great variety of policy-formulation arenas in the American political system. They include political parties, the Congress, the President, the federal bureaucracy and other formal decision-making councils, individual interest groups, and amalgamations of actors on an ad-hoc basis from these and other institutions.

An issue that is spawned within an initial policy formulation arena, that is accepted by a community, and is backed by sufficient power, may be channelized with little difficulty into the formal decision-making arena. Another issue may penetrate the formal arena only if it gains sufficient public attention to generate widespread support for its resolution by policy-makers. When this occurs, and the "scope of conflict" expands, the clash of interests often centers on who is to control the formulation of the issue rather than on how the issue should be resolved. Under these circumstances the power-wielder within the initial issue-formulation arena may well lose control of the ultimate shape and nature of the issue. Clearly it is to his advantage to confine the issue within the initial formulation arena, providing, of course, that in so doing he is able to press successfully for its resolution within the original decision-making arena.[6]

The Population Coalition

The Population Coalition is the arena in which population policy has been, and currently is being, formulated. It is a coalition of individuals and institutions that have assumed identifiable and distinctive roles in the process of population policy-making. They are linked together by both common interests and objectives, and by cooperative activities in pursuit of these objectives.

The Population Coalition embodies three distinctive roles. The first is concerned with the illumination and conceptualization of population issues, the application of scientific methodology to them, and the translation of scientific findings into remedies susceptible to application. This role is performed by specialists with the requisite intellectual capacities and professional credentials. The group is accordingly characterized as the Professional/Intellectuals. Its distinctive contribution is a resource that is characterized as Cerebral. It is the intellectual core of the American population coalition.

The membership of this core is based in the university system, with key outposts in the foundations and the federal bureaucracy. In the universities they are clustered around departments of sociology, schools of medicine and public health, and population centers, which provide the institutional focus for research and training activities in population matters. In the foundations, they staff the units that design activities and allocate resources for population enterprises. And in the public bureaucracy, they are found in official and advisory capacities, from which decisions are made about programs and funding. In its ranging institutional scope and potential influence in the establishment of goals and allocation of the relevant resources, the intellectual core might qualify as a miniature academic/bureaucratic counterpart to the military/industrial complex in another policy area.

The second role is concerned with providing selected remedies the initial support, both financial and political, and privileged or priority status on a policy agenda. This role is performed by persons in the community of stature and influence, derived from their professional success, social status, wealth, and other sources of preeminence. They function in their private capacities. The group is accordingly characterized as the Private Influentials. Their contribution is a resource described as Influence.

The private influential arm is composed of the civic leaders, and the economic and professional notables who serve as officers, board members, and just plain members of the foundations, associations, and other institutions concerned with population issues. Their principal contribution is the legitimization of the Coalition's objectives within the national community, as a result of lending their prestige and influence to them. The members of this sector are concerned with staking a claim to resources, and making good the claim by exercising the necessary influence through appropriate channels. Personal preeminence and communal recognition comprise their principal armament. The private influential arm might qualify as the Population Coalition's version of the "old boy network."[7]

The third role is concerned with providing the formal authority and the public financial resources for development and application of the remedies. This role is performed by officers of the government, in both the legislative and executive branches. The group accordingly is described as the Public Official sector. The members of this sector dispose over two resources, a principal product which is authority, and a collateral one which is money.

The Public Official sector is comprised of the public functionaries: the bureaucrats, legislators and their staffs, who pass and execute the laws that create and establish the federal government's position in population issues. They are located principally in the United States Congress; the Executive Office of the President; the Department of Health, Education and Welfare and its appendages; and in the Agency for International Development.

The public officials function as the resource center of the coalition. They are its principal provisioners in providing the inputs of public authority and public funding. And, in a formal sense, they are supposed to be most representative of the public interest by serving as a receptacle for signals of relevant needs and wants originating in the community. Official position, the related access to levers of power, and a disposition over public funds constitute their main contribution. A more detailed discussion of the coalition's structure follows in Chapter 4.

Decisions and Non-Decisions

The subsequent analysis of the Population Coalition is based upon the mutual reinforcement of two concepts: *mobilization of bias and non-decision-making.*

"All forms of political organization," Schattschneider declared, "have a bias in favor of the exploitation of some kinds of conflict and the suppression of others because organization is the mobilization of bias. Some issues are organized into politics while others are organized out."[8] The concept of *mobilization of bias* is useful in public policy analysis because it underscores a perspective all too often neglected: what is not on the agenda of government is as significant as what is on the agenda; what governments do not do may well be as important as what they do.

It is clear, for example, that the prevailing procedures, values, and attitudes in politics operate—leaving open the question of to what degree of intentionality—to advantage some and disadvantage others. If numbers of supporters is an important resource in American democracy, then interests commanding the support of only a few—other things being equal—are at a disadvantage. If wealth is an approved political resource but violence is not, then interests commanding the former enjoy an advantage as compared to interests with a capacity to undertake the latter.

So, too, with prevailing institutional arrangements. The fragmentation of political power embodied in, among other things, the separation of powers, checks and balances, and federalism, provides differential advantages to various interest groupings in American society. A non-partisan local election, for example, structures political access and influence differently from a partisan election.

Since the prevailing configuration of bias in a political system both reflects and legitimizes the existing distribution of power within the system, it is difficult for groups outside of the system's ideological boundaries to gain entry and to marshall enough power to introduce new biases and to determine and shape new issues for consideration within the system. As Jack Walker has observed, "The agenda of controversy, the list of questions which are recognized by the active participants in politics as legitimate subjects of attention and concern, is very hard to change."[9] Not only is legitimacy a powerful resource for perpetuating the *status quo*, but the preferred position awarded to well-organized groups within a loosely-knit political system also creates a powerful bulwark against change.[10]

In observing the relationship between legitimacy and group power in the United States, Theodore Lowi depicts a corporate policy-making structure in American politics wherein the competition of ideas and preferences in discrete policy areas is circumscribed because the dominant role in policy-making is parceled out to the groups who successfully lay claim to the objects affected by the policy-making involved. Once the allocation of policy-making power in respective areas of interest is accomplished, the groups principally interested in each stay off each other's back.[11]

A pronounced mobilization of bias, whether characteristic of the total political system, or a piece of it, such as a particular policy area, leads to and is reinforced by non-decision-making. A non-decision, as indicated above, is a decision that results in suppression or thwarting of a latent or manifest challenge to the values or interests of the principal decision-maker.

Non-decision-making, which is a significant technique of policy formulation, may assume one of several forms. One form, although indirect, attempts to reshape or strengthen the mobilization of bias as a precautionary measure to block future challenges to the prevailing allocation of values and choices. This variation is a tactic that reinforces existing barriers or constructs new ones to frustrate efforts that might expand the policy-formulation arena by the incorporation of new approaches and ideas, and new and diverse participants. By reinforcing the prevailing allocation of values in a particular policy area, non-decision-making also discourages excluded groups from attempting to establish competing arenas for formulating policy about the subject matter at stake.

Another and more direct form of non-decision-making invokes an existing bias of the system—a norm, precedent, rule, or procedure—to squelch a new or competitive demand, or an incipient issue. This form employs an exercise of power that is utilized to police a system. In a policy-making process, this type of non-decision-making would be a direct attempt to forestall an existing challenge to the dominant interests and aims.

While the first type of non-decision may be described as a positive exercise of power, with the aim of strengthening or augmenting an existing structure, the second type is negative, since its purpose is to prevent "foreign" intrusion into the system. The exercise of power manifested in either form of non-decision-making is motivated by a desire to protect or strengthen a particular mobilization of bias.[12]

There has been considerable criticism of the non-decision-making concept on the ground that a non-decision is not susceptible to empirical study, since a non-decision, when it is most effective, disallows conflict.[13] The result, it is said, is a non-event. A non-event is non-empirical; therefore the concept of non-decision-making has little value for the serious student of political power. The difficulty with this criticism is that although the absence of conflict may be a non-event, the prevention of conflict *is* an event. And such an event, as an exercise of power either to suppress or support a particular interpretation of an issue, is subject to observation and analysis, and certainly to critical scrutiny. In the course of this essay several important instances of non-decision-making are examined. We defer to the reader to judge for himself the usefulness of this concept, whatever its susceptibility to empirical validation.

Technocratic and Representative Policy-Making

Within this conceptual framework the analysis is focused upon several inter-related questions: Does a mobilization of bias actually exist within the Population Coalition which constrains the policy discourse on population issues by influencing the scope and nature of population research, the allocation of funds for research, and the issues that are posed for decision by policy-makers? If such a bias exists, do certain participants in the policy process enjoy a preferred position to utilize power to defend and promote their interests and the goals they espouse? And if so, what, if any, interests are excluded, and policy options ignored or turned aside?

Historically, policy-makers have been dependent upon others for information upon which to act. Students of the American Presidency, for example, cannot fail to be impressed by the tendency of subordinates within the bureaucracy to make their own decisions about the policy options and data that should be presented or withheld from the President.

In recent years the rapid development of technology and the increasing complexity and seriousness of social problems have added another dimension to the shift of power in policy-making from elected representatives to experts. There has been a significant increase in the reliance upon analyses and findings of outside experts, including social scientists, in the formulation of public policy. Indeed, by their predigestion and technical sorting out of the issues and boundaries, and selection of the related pertinent data and techniques for analysis, experts in effect engage in pre-decision-making. To the extent that it exists, this process could relegate to the formal policy-makers in government the task of legitimizing the policy preferences of a cadre of "invisible elites."[14] We are concerned that this type of pre-decision-making by a technocratic elite is a significant characteristic in American population policy-formulation.

What is particularly dangerous about this phenomenon, if indeed it exists, is not only its inconsistency with the norms of American representative democracy, but also its misleading apolitical character. In treating political issues in the guise of scientific problems, the expert, armed with his scientific jargon and supporting data, can give the appearance of proposing dispassionate solutions which are devoid of political bias.[15] In fact, in the selection of problems and the related means of analysis, the technocrat is no less susceptible to introducing his own political bias than is the politician or the private citizen. Equally important the technocrat can escape political accountability for the essentially political solutions he proposes. He may easily claim immunity from accountability by virtue of expertise. What may prove to be the most pernicious aspect of policy-making by technocrats is the exclusion of diverse policy options that might emerge from the viewpoints and diverse preferences of the unexpert lay public. In this age of expertise, the lay public, and the politician as well, can too easily be overwhelmed by the technocrat. Beyond the stifling of uneducated and unscientific preferences in the community-at-large, pre-decision-making by technocrats can suppress unorthodox viewpoints within the community of experts.

We confess to a political bias that the primary function of a democratic polity is to enable the greatest number of people to participate in making choices about their lives and the condition of their society. At a minimum, the polity must provide the citizenry with the necessary means to make rational choices. These include such things as information, education, security, opportunities to earn a livelihood, and the channels through which choices can be freely expressed and made effective.

As life in the technological age becomes more complex, the process of choice-making also becomes more complex and difficult. Admittedly the resolution of major issues confronting American society requires expert knowledge and the application of advanced technology and science. But this requirement does not mean that choices among values inevitably underlying alternative technological solutions should be made only by experts and not by ordinary citizens. The professional is prone to link his ability to perform services with an obligation to make value judgments about how the services should be rendered and for what purpose. Ironically, this position is often reinforced by the ordinary citizen, who abdicates his responsibility to take a stand on a policy issue on the ground that the problem is too complex and technical, and thus had best be left to the judgment of the expert.

We are disturbed by this inadequate style of choice-making. all the more so in those areas in which the stakes are so high. American population policy is such an area.

Part I:
The Substance of Policy
Formulation

2

The Politicization of Ecology

The Population Spectre

The concept of population growth propounded by the Reverend Thomas Malthus 200 years ago has provided the major impetus for current anxieties about the consequences of population growth. Population, when unchecked, increases in a geometric ratio. Subsistence, however, increases only in an arithmetic ratio.[1] The issue posed by Malthus, and resurrected today, is how to reconcile unlimited population growth with the physical limitations of a finite globe.

Technological breakthroughs have created this dilemma; their uneven distribution has compounded it. The impact of new health technologies in developing countries has resulted in a dramatic decline in death rates which once negated high birth rates. Now, birth rates have overtaken death rates, and as a result, population in developing nations is doubling every twenty to thirty years. Thus, there are more people around, especially between the ages of one and fifteen, to feed, clothe, house, educate, and, in general, to satisfy.

In developed countries such as the United States, the growth and concentration of population has generated an even more complex order of concerns about how the increasing advantages of developed societies can continue to be enjoyed by more people. The United States has discovered the pollution of air, land, and water. Moving from one place to another in the large metropolitan areas is increasingly difficult, as a result of traffic congestion. Recreational facilities are overcrowded. Classrooms have too many children. Welfare costs continue to rise. And the demands for public services imposed on the American states, counties, and cities as a result of these conditions threaten to convulse them.

While Malthus was correct in postulating that people tend to multiply exponentially, he failed to recognize that the food supply would also increase exponentially. Due to developments in agricultural technology in recent years, production of foodstuffs has grown at a substantially higher rate than world population. As a consequence of the Green Revolution, poorer nations such as Indonesia and Pakistan can produce sufficient grains and cereals to feed their populations.[2]

Malthus also failed to anticipate the impact of rising standards of living upon the behavioral patterns of industrial societies. It is now evident that as a nation becomes more prosperous, people tend to limit the size of their families. Despite these critical oversights, however, Malthus was prescient in citing the problem of unlimited population increase in a finite universe.

11

The Emerging Issue

Confidence in technological progress was a major influence in the prescriptive remedies devised for dealing with population growth during the past two decades. A more profound understanding of the human reproductive system, coupled with breakthroughs in contraceptive technology, produced the loop and the pill. The availability of these products permitted the planning of widespread fertility control programs on a scale hitherto unattainable in both developed and less developed societies. These contraceptive materials and their widespread dissemination could achieve an early impact on fertility and, ultimately, on population growth. And the use of these new products was consistent with traditional attitudes regarding decisions about contraception. The loop and the pill would be employed by individual females who themselves would decide on when and if they wanted not to conceive. The materials would merely be made available to facilitate individual decisions about the planning of families.

This process of coupling individual decisions about fertility with the easy availability of effective contraceptive materials is the core of the traditional family-planning ideology in the United States. Accordingly, this formula was an attractive one for Americans who were taking an interest in promoting a global slowdown of population growth.

The preamble of the Family Planning and Population Services Act of 1970 expresses the essence of the family-planning ideology, which is based on the desirability of expanding individual freedom of choice in fertility decision-making:

> ... unwanted births impair the stability and well-being of the individual family and severely limit the opportunity of each child within the family ... over five million women (American) are denied access to modern, effective, medically safe family planning services due to financial need ... family planning has been recognized nationally and internationally as a universal human right ... it is the policy of Congress to foster the integrity of the family and opportunity for each child; to guarantee the right of the family to freely determine the number and spacing of its children within the dictates of its individual consciences; to extend family planning services, on a voluntary basis, to all who desire such services.[3]

The advocates of the individualized family-planning approach maintain that parents should continue to be unrestrained in their decisions about family size. Population growth problems can be corrected by providing families with sufficient contraceptive information and devices so they can effectively control the numbers of their progeny.[4]

Family-planning organizations, among other measures, have established birth control clinics on an international basis that make information and technology available to all persons who are not using effective contraceptive methods. These public-funded family-planning programs are designed primarily for the uneducated and the poor. However, as the individualized family-planning remedy was put into operation, experience revealed that it would not achieve the desired impact on population growth rates as quickly as might be desired, particularly in underdeveloped countries.[5] Accordingly, another set of prescriptions evolved that used family planning as the first stage, but then ventured considerably beyond it.

In common with family planning, these approaches which are called *population planning*, focused on individual fertility as the object for manipulation. But unlike family planning, which relied upon individual choice on a voluntary basis, the population-planning approaches introduced society as a legitimate participant in influencing individual choices. The population-planning remedies were based on the assumption that the community as a whole has an interest in individual fertility choices, and that the community, through its established institutions, should have the opportunity to influence these choices. Beyond this ideological base, the population planners maintain that the individualized family-planning remedy has proven inadequate in influencing population growth. Thus, if an impact on population growth is the objective, remedies of more global character are required for its achievement.

There are two identifiable streams of the population-planning approach. One maintains that fertility is influenced principally by conditions of social and economic development. Improvement in these conditions results in lower fertility. To the extent that this position suggests deliberate government influencing of fertility to ameliorate population growth, it maintains such intervention is appropriate only in accordance with the preferences and rights of individual members of society.[6]

The second stream assumes that direct political intervention in individual choices is required for the welfare of society. Advocates of this position raise two basic objections to the individualized family-planning approach: (1) significant segments of the population may resist using the technology; and (2) even widespread acceptance of the technology would result in little or no decline in population growth—that is, families may use the contraceptives to plan for three, four, five or more children. This position embodies remedies that would effectively compel individuals to employ contraceptive technology.

The argument that individual choice to procreate must be limited to assure present and future generations the right to enjoy lives free from overcrowding, hunger, and pollution is expressed in Garret Hardin's portrayal of the world's ecosystem as a common pasture. He argues that if individuals guided solely by personal preferences increase their own herd the pasture will be ruined for all. He therefore concludes that if the "Common" is to be utilized for the maximum opportunity and enjoyment of all, freedom to breed must be constrained and regulated by society.[7] And if breeding cannot be limited in all societies, Hardin suggests that at least a few pastures should be enclosed:

In a less than perfect world, the allocation of rights based on territory must be defended if a ruinous breeding race is to be avoided. It is unlikely that civilization and dignity can survive everywhere; but better in a few places than in none. Fortunate minorities must act as the trustees of a civilization that is threatened by uninformed good intentions.[8]

The direct intervention required to discourage breeding is formulated within a wide range of remedies. The socialization process as it relates to family size would be revamped. Pronatalist policies that are currently being underwritten by public authorities would be repealed in favor of antinatalist measures. These would include a tax structure that discriminates against large families, sterilization licenses, and government-sponsored abortion facilities.[9]

More bold and direct measures have been proposed. In *Beyond Conception*, Martha K. Willing would label as criminal any couple who procreate more than themselves, and Edgar Chasteen proposes "inoculating" males and females against fertility at puberty.[10]

A Global Framework

During the past five years, the discourse on population planning has been enriched and enlivened by new participants who contributed a scientific articulation of how population growth might affect man's opportunity for survival on a finite globe. Their agenda involved issues no longer confined to the manipulation of fertility under varying conditions, but rather to the question of survival itself. The new participants are a group of scientists from outside the heretofore traditional population mix of demography and public health specialists who combined scientific rigor with social consciousness in dealing with the issues. Their concern arrived at the right time and the right place within an atmosphere of increasing sensitivity among influential segments of American opinion about the ecological and environmental future.

In this climate of concern, the work of the new spokesmen escaped the obscurity of scientific journals to which it might otherwise have been confined, and emerged on best-seller lists. Thus, the publications of Commoner, Ehrlich, and the Meadows group have been widely reviewed, publicized, and discussed in the media, among public groups, and within the intellectual community.[11] Taken together, these works represent a variety of concerns, each reflecting distinctive normative and intellectual approaches. But, in common, they all address the issue of human and social survival, and the conditions under which men and societies would live. Within this common framework the issue of population growth represents a major consideration.

Our discussion here of ecological and environmental issues does not refer to the limited version of this discourse which has been popularized during recent years in pleas to save the bald eagle, the blue whale, and the Oregon coastline. This is not what a true environmental debate is all about. The preoccupation with these superficial symptoms of environmental deterioration, and their elevation into objects for public crusading, distorts a meaningful encounter with real environmental issues. Thus Philip Hauser has observed:

> ... there is danger that the ecologists' crusade ... can be used as a smokescreen to obscure more immediate and pressing man-made environmental problems of at least equally high priority. Certainly in the coming generation it will be at least as important to eliminate slums and ghettos as to preserve the Great Lakes; and to eliminate rats in substandard housing as to preserve the bald eagle.[12]

A meaningful environmental discourse, illustrated by examples in this chapter, involves a global perspective on environmental issues which raises basic questions about man's encounter with his physical surroundings and how this encounter influences and is influenced by the reciprocal relationships of men, societies, and physical surroundings.

Our analysis is focused on the quality of these scientific contributions as ingredients in the American population policy-making process. Beyond their treatment of technological issues we are particularly interested in their treatment of relevant political factors in developing their analyses and reaching their conclusions. We are also interested in whether the scientists involved have recognized the political conditions that intervene between their conclusions and the policies they recommend, and, specifically, who should be involved in evaluating the related policy choices, and with what possible consequences. Finally, we will speculate on how this provocative new group of concerns was treated by the first national commission concerned with American population policy formation (The Commission on Population Growth and the American Future).

The ecological perspective on population planning considers population growth and size in relation to resource depletion and utilization of the environment. This expanded approach maintains that it is not only the pressures of population, but also wealth that endangers the environment. The Malthusian formula is reversed—the poor are not the cause of "overpopulating"; rather, the rich. Thus, although the birth rate and population density in the United States appears to be stabilizing and is relatively low compared to Latin America, Africa, and Asia, the United States is still one of the most overpopulated countries on the Earth. Though the United States population is approximately less than 6 percent of the world's total, it is claimed that Americans deplete 40 percent of the non-renewable resources, and, furthermore, excessively poison the world's ecosystem at the rate of 30 percent.[13]

Because they see the devastating impact of an affluent society upon the ecological balance, Ehrlich and others argue that economic growth must be stabilized at a rate of zero. In Ehrlich's words,

> "A massive campaign must be launched to restore a quality environment in North America and to *de-develop the U.S.*"[14]

Restructuring the economy on a low consumption level that is in accord with the natural global balance would create mammoth political problems. Ehrlich rightly wonders whether a capitalist system is dependent upon continuing expansion, and if this expansion will eventually necessitate a radical redistribution of wealth.[15]

Lady Barbara Ward Jackson, author of the official background report for the United Nations Environmental Conference in Stockholm, notes that enrivonmental collapse ensues when three-fourths of the world's resources are controlled and wasted by the industrialized one-fourth.[16] Confronted with facts such as these, Ehrlich, advocates a more equitable distribution of income among peoples throughout the world. Yet he avoids dealing with the profound political dislocations which such reform inevitably would require. Leaving these issues aside, Ehrlich emphasizes that population *control* must be an immediate policy objective to alleviate the environmental crises.[17]

As for underdeveloped countries replicating the modernization tracks of their industrialized predecessors, Ehrlich maintains the industrialization of underdeveloped countries would be the most threatening detriment to ecological stability. Lady Ward Jackson supports this position. "If these results (waste, pollution, etc.) follow from the high standards of one-fourth of humanity, what might happen to planet Earth if three-fourths sought the same level of income?"[18] Ehrlich proposes a plan for "ecologically sensible agricultural development with supporting facilities for distribution, marketing and storage— i.e., semi-development." However, the institution of this system is dependent on a significant alteration in the developed-underdeveloped country relationship.[19] The disparity between the two worlds requires correction through more equitable and open channels of discussion concerning foreign aid, mutual development, and international politics. Echoing Ehrlich's views, C.P. Snow of Great Britain and Dr. Andrei Sakharov suggest that industrialized nations contribute "20 percent of their GNP for ten to fifteen years to the task of population control and economic development of the poor countries."[20] Here again, Ehrlich's ecological analysis leads directly to fundamental issues of political transformation.

In his widely read book *The Closing Circle*, Commoner challenges Ehrlich's thesis. He contends that technology and contemporary modes of production, not population growth, are the primary culprits of environmental deterioration.[21] Although their respective positions maintain that population size, affluence, and technology are all contributors to the mix of environmental deterioration, Ehrlich, following the Malthusian lead, regards population growth as the most detrimental, while Commoner maintains "I have found that the numerical size of such technological changes...was much larger than the concurrent increase in population...and on these grounds suggested that it might be wrong to conclude that the environmental crisis is exclusively, or even chiefly, the result of population growth."[22]

Commoner would not suggest a return to "primitive conditions" to achieve a state of zero environmental impact, but rather the need for "technological advancements that are biologically and ecologically safe."[23] The achievement of this state would require, he believes, the elimination of the exploitation of resources for private profit and a drastic transition in wasteful technology and the means of production. He presents statistical evidence which he claims demonstrates that waste and overproduction, not population, place primary stress on the ecosystem. An ecologically sensible means of industrialization would permit increased economic growth without a corresponding increase in pollution. An ecologically stable industrialization is consistent with a more productive economy and higher standards of living. This process would have a major impact in reducing birth rates.[24]

In contending that the ecosystem capable of sustaining human life can survive only if counter-ecological productive technology is instituted, Commoner concludes that the private enterprise system in the United States must undergo a parametric change.[25] Owing to the magnitude of this required change, he believes it improbable that government and industry would be willing to support it unless compelled to do so by strong and persistent pressure from environmental organizations and the public. Such action requires "that the people ... become familiar with the basic facts of environmental deterioration, become aware of alternative interpretations ... and then undertake the difficult task of weighing this information ... against their own ethical, social, and political beliefs in order to determine what must be done."[26]

Commoner also believes that policy-formulation and decision-making about ecological and population matters relating to developing nations can no longer be delegated to powerful elites. The continuation of this style of decision-making would permanently relegate the poorer nations to second-class economic and political status. Although he has no suggestions as to how to right the power balance between have and have-not nations, Commoner stresses that industrialization of developing nations—in accord with ecological guidelines—is the only lasting solution to the problem. In sharp contrast to Ehrlich, who relies heavily on population controls to curb excessive population growth, Commoner would depend on "self-made decisions to limit fertility, which people reach because they have confidence in their future."[27] His position rests on the crucial requirement that social action will be forthcoming with sufficient vigor and enlightenment to provide the basis for a secure and productive life for all people.

Cataclysm Via Computer

The gloomy projections of the MIT computer study, *The Limits of Growth,*[28] augment the Ehrlich-Commoner controversy. The message is unequivocal: Growth must come to a halt and soon, or mankind faces an uncontrollable and

disastrous collapse within the next hundred years. The study calls for stabilization of both the world's population and economy within the next few decades.
However, it emphasizes that these measures alone are not sufficient. Despite zero
growth in population and the economy, resource shortages will sooner or later
develop, reducing industrial output and disrupting the temporary equilibrium.[29]
Thus, additional measures required to sustain life without endangering the
world's ecology would include:

1. Sharp curtailment in resource consumption and in pollution per unit of
   industrial output;
2. Further reduction of resource depletion and pollution, preferential expansion of services—such as education and health—at the expense of factory-
   produced material goods;
3. Accommodation to the well-being of all people in a stabilized world by
   means of distribution of goods and services to all at an average income rate
   of roughly $1,800 per capita—an amount equal to the present average
   European income, but three times the present average world income, and
   about one-half the present average U.S. income.[30]

The validity of the study has been challenged for its neglect of the ability of
continuing technological advances, such as wider use of nuclear power, to extend
significantly the limits of economic and population growth.[31] To meet this
objection, the MIT team assumed that the "technological optimists" were
correct and that the resource problems of the world would be solved by the use
of nuclear energy. Their computer run found, however, that "unlimited"
resources were no solution.[32] An inexhaustible resource supply, they maintain,
facilitates a continuing rise of industrial production, but would in turn threaten
the entire ecological system by causing an intolerable level of pollution.

Even assuming a strict pollution-control system whereby the rate of pollution
per unit of output is reduced by a factor of four, a pollution crisis would
develop as the world's production increases fourfold.[33]

On a more philosophic note the authors lament that man's successful
encounter with technology in the past has blinded him to the possibility that
future technological advances will be incompatible with a life-supporting
ecosystem. Rather than continuing to fight against limits, the authors argue that
man now must learn to live with them.[34]

The MIT team maintains that the "technological optimist" refuses to face up
to the hard reality that "the application of technology to apparent problems of
resource depletion or pollution or food shortage has no impact on the essential
problem, which is expotential growth in an infinite and complex system."[35]

The team poses a key challenge: "Is it better," the authors ask, "to try to live
within existing ecological limits by accepting a self-imposed restriction on
growth? Or is it preferable to go on growing until some other natural limits arise,
in the hope that at that time another technological leap will allow further
growth to continue still longer?"[36]

The *Limits of Growth* study, however evaluated, neglects some fundamental political questions intimately related to the prognosis. Among the most significant are the political consequences of the challenge to a long-held expectation that better conditions of life for deprived groups in the world can be obtained by continuing the present patterns of growth. What happens to the visions of more just and egalitarian societies based on the growth premise? To the extent they have them, would deprived mass publics be willing to abandon their expectations of a better life? What sorts of substantial political changes are required to limit growth? Such changes most likely would require a substantial reordering of power relationships among classes, groups, and peoples in nations and among nations. But who would initiate these substantial changes and make the related decisions to install them? In other words, who could decide to stop growth and how?

And once a no-growth society emerges, the basic issue of how values are allocated and who receives them could no longer be glossed over by appeals to growth. In the words of Herman Daly:

The argument that everyone should be happy as long as his absolute share of wealth increases, regardless of his relative share, will no longer be available. . . . The stationary state would make fewer demands on our environmental resources, but much greater demands on our moral resources.[37]

Whatever the deficiencies in scope and method, the *Limits* study has achieved considerable public impact. For example, at the close of the United Nations Environmental Conference, Margaret Mead read a statement that had a similar ring to it:

So great has been the technological thrust of our science and energy, so repetitious our consumption of non-renewable resources, so rapid our growth in numbers, so heavy the load we place on our life-supporting systems that we begin to perceive the infinite qualities of the biosphere of soil and water. . . . This is a revolution in thought fully compatible to the Copernican revolution.[38]

The Dissident Deprived

Some of the political waves that might be anticipated in reaction to the *Limits of Growth* analysis are suggested by positions on the relationships between population growth and development that already have emerged in developing societies of the world, both abroad and in the U.S. These positions are not satisfactorily addressed by purely technological discussions. The suggestion of population and environmental controls—especially those that would restrain industrial development—are viewed by developing countries as measures to prevent them from emulating the economic and technological development of the West. At the United Nations Environmental Conference in Stockholm, a Brazilian delegate put it cogently: "Brazil will not allow ecological concerns to prejudice her economic development."[39]

At the African Population Conference in Accra in December 1971, a group of African intellectuals issued an attack on population control in a document entitled *A New Approach to Population Research in Africa: Ideologies, Facts and Politics.* They maintained that deliberate curtailment of their high population-growth rates would contradict their national interests, while fostering what they described as the vested interests of "exporters and nations that dominate the world economy."[40] They assert that "the neo-Malthusian thesis in no way corresponds to reality, but to a conscious or unconscious ideological position. This thesis is characterized by 'population fetichism,' that is the consideration of population itself, unsituated in a framework of complex relationships."[41] They maintain that economic exploitation of the masses is the prime cause of rapid population growth, and that it is evidenced in ways including inadequate nutrition and health facilities, which result in a high mortality rate, especially for infants. The masses thus overpopulate in order to assure an adult generation.[42]

Further, the African group suggests that a widespread feeling of insecurity, as graphically illustrated by high unemployment, encourages people to foster procreation as a form of social security. To deal with the population problem, while neglecting the socioeconomic malady, they claim, is the unintelligent assignment of Western over Third World priorities. They charge that family planning or control measures cannot substantially ease the economic conditions in Africa, while industrial development is continually hindered by the pseudo-mercantilist theories that have been promulgated by colonialists.

Population control, in their view, is merely a penumbra. Until the underdeveloped countries of Africa, South America, and Asia can attain freedom from industrial encroachments and manage their resources to the benefits of their peoples, the present economic and population inequities will prevail.[43]

A variation of the African theme is expressed by Latin American leaders.[44] Here again the argument is made that population control is a vestige of colonialism, mostly American, that seeks to suppress independent development in the Latin American countries. Stycos documents these positions in a recent analysis of foreign resistance to birth control.[45] As a solution to their development malaise, many of those leaders favor growth and development, and a more effective system for distributing the rewards of the development process.

The reservations about population control expressed by a less developed enclave of American society are similar to those originating in less developed countries. Black Americans, militants and moderates, suspect that the ecology and population movements are marketing a smokescreen to stifle their struggle for a more just distribution of advantages. While deterioration of the environment is a serious problem, they argue, it is a distortion of priorities to elevate it to crisis status when the black community continues to suffer from widespread deprivation. They regard the focus on ecological and population reforms designed to enhance the quality of life for posterity as a tactic to obscure the more fundamental and immediate problem of reconstructing society to provide decent lives and freedom for the present generation. They view the population problem as the maldistribution of opportunities among a deprived population, caused by exploitation and continued discrimination.[46]

This concern was expressed by the Reverend Jesse Jackson, testifying before The Commission of Population Growth and the American Future in Chicago in 1971. He said the problem is not population growth, but distribution of resources, wealth, and raw materials. Noting concerns among some that increasing population will consume too much in the way of resources, Jackson said, "the heaviest concentrations of population are not those who are consuming the earth's substance. Disparities in income and wealth, not disproportions of population, are the real source of our problems."

Jackson said that this nation needs a Hunger Commission, not a Population Commission, and that the United States has the wealth and resources to care for its population easily, if it only chose to do so. He added that the question of population is low among the priorities in the black community because there are so many other more pressing needs, such as poverty, employment, housing, education, health care, etc. He said that when the question is raised, it is viewed with suspicion out of fear that it is an effort to curtail the black community. "Virtually all of our logical security is in the number of children we produce," Jackson said, noting that it has been the development of black majorities which have led to the election of black public officials in major cities.[47]

As long as they see the race issue eclipsed by public concerns about ecological and population problems, it is reasonable for blacks to continue their hostile stance against family planning programs and population control policies. Not only do they see the latter competing with the racial issue for public attention and a place on legislative and administrative agendas, but they fear compliance by the black community in programs designed to decrease growth would have an adverse impact in lessening potential pressure for basic social change. But, like Jackson, they argue that a relative increase in the fertility rate of a subpopulation enhances its potential source of power within the electoral arena, and thus creates a power resource to sustain a strategy of protest.

Their premise has some basis in fact; for, a shift in the composition of any population in favor of youth is likely to produce new and fertile sources of protest against the *status quo*.[48] This possibility could be recognized by young blacks who have become increasingly hostile to white society, and who envision the production of a self-confident new generation which would become a major force for social change.

The common argument that large families are debilitating to the poor misses the point. The strategy of the black militant is not directed toward amelioration of individual suffering. It is, rather, designed to build a "power base" that will be instrumental in releasing an entire group from its present condition of deprivation.[49] Thus, a pronatalist policy is a key ingredient of the black militant strategy.

The Dissident Scientists

The position of the ecological survivalists represents neither a consensus among their scientific peers, nor does it reflect the preferences of peoples whose processes of development their remedies would restrain. Developing societies seem to be saying, "Give us something better that is worth preserving, then we will worry about how to preserve it." And there are members of the scientific community who do not consider this position unreasonable.

The critical significance of development and a more equitable distribution of its rewards in the developing countries is seen by some Western scientists as the most effective route to mediating excessive population growth. Thus Roger Revelle visualizes poverty, injustice, and economic insecurity as the principal causes as well as the consequences of rapid population growth. He is persuaded that a pattern of economic and social development in these countries is the only effective remedy for overpopulation. Revelle suggests that a reordered social environment is a prerequisite for a liveable physical environment. Accordingly, he suggests the priority need to address issues of modernization.

Some writers have suggested that the world's natural resources, especially of metals and of energy, are so limited that large-scale industrialization of the poor countries is not possible, and, even if it were, the resulting global pollution would be intolerable. The corollary is that many less developed countries can at best be only partially developed and must remain largely agricultural. Something like this "semi-development" may actually happen during the next few decades in many poor countries, but over the long run the proposal contains fatal flaws. First is the difficulty of convincing the people of the poor countries that they must forever remain second-class citizens in the world society.

Second, the proposal completely neglects the cities, which will probably contain more than half the populations of the less developed countries by the year 2000.

Third, profound social change is the most basic consequence of rapid population growth. The people of the poor countries have already made a fundamental change in their traditional way of life by accepting, indeed wholeheartedly welcoming, the great increases in life expectancy that result from Western technology. They are more likely to accept population control if they experience a marked improvement in economic and social conditions, because this improvement raises the "opportunity costs" of having many children by greatly increasing the possibilities for social mobility. Fourth, the inevitable growth of population during the next few decades will mean that a large proportion of the labor force must find employment outside the agricultural sector. Finally, as we have seen, sustained agricultural improvement will be extremely difficult in most countries without overall economic and social development outside agriculture.[50]

Barry Commoner, too, supports this position by arguing that the central issue is not population control vs. family planning, but rather "increased food production and economic development which brings about higher productivity and, therefore, a higher standard of living."[51] This end result, coupled with a reduction in infant mortality rates, not only will implement the objective of fertility reduction, but will also be a vital means of absorbing widespread unemployment.[52] Further, economic development is essential to sustain the agricultural improvements that will accompany the inevitable increases in population.

Revelle speculates on the unique developmental processes that developing countries are likely to experience. Developing countries will be forced to adopt radically non-Western methods of industrialization and utilization of available materials. Instead of relying on coal or oil, which are in limited supply at present, developing countries will draw upon the almost infinite reservoir of nuclear power and even, perhaps, some new, yet undiscovered power.[53]

In contrast to Ehrlich, Revelle does not foresee any devastating effects of this process on the ecosystem from the economic development of the Third World. However, he does conclude that "helping the poor countries to build up their own new industries, in which anti-pollution measures might be incorporated from the beginning" is less expensive and ecologically more feasible than the mere expenditure of foreign aid.[54]

This position was reinforced throughout the UN Conference on the Human Environment. A prevailing theme was that "sound economic development and environmental quality were not only compatible, but were inextricable." R.E. Train, Chairman of the U.S. delegation, explained: "We are learning that it is far less costly and more effective to build the necessary environmental quality into new plants and new communities from the outset than it is to rebuild or modify old facilities. The time to do the job of environmental protection is at the outset, not later. This holds true for every country at every stage of development."[55]

If this goal is to be achieved, the conflicts of interest between developed and underdeveloped countries must be reconciled to the collective end of harmonizing environmental and economic aspirations. This is a utopian notion; especially when contrasted to the lack of evidence that the developed countries, especially the U.S. and the U.S.S.R., intend to abandon their continued expansion and relinquish a larger portion of the world's industry and economy to benefit underdeveloped nations.[56] Nor does available evidence suggest that wealthier governments will generously contribute increased levels of foreign aid.

Perhaps, as Kingsley Davis suggests, radical change in underdeveloped countries is requisite to rapid industrialization and changing social patterns.[57] The symptoms of decline in population growth and the changing attitudes toward large families in the aftermath of revolution in China and Cuba illustrate the potential merit of Davis' position.

In any case, there are scientists who have suggested that an effective alternative, other than restraining or turning back the modernization process, is available for developing countries.

The Critical Omission

Despite the visions of a better society they both express and imply, those who would restrain development or curtail growth—let us label them "the ecologists"—neglect the potential influence of political change that would affect both their visions and the calculations that produce them. They start with conditions of life as we know them today and project them forward into some future time. They develop complex interrelationships projecting forward population conditions as we know them today, limitations of natural resources as we see them today, patterns of production and consumption as we experience them today, and systems of political and social life that exist today. From an analysis of this mix they arrive at recommendations for de-development or redevelopment.

However, they exclude the possibility that a different series of production and consumption relationships might emerge from substantial political change in individual societies, and the world as a whole, with the related changes in distribution of power and advantages. How would radical political upheaval, for example, affect the availability of resources, their distribution, the patterns of production and consumption, and, incidentally, the growth of population? What might be the reciprocal influence of these factors on one another? Granted that prospects of political change are difficult to quantify, and resist the more rigorous forms of scientific analysis, but for any meaningful speculation about future conditions of man and society, they must be considered.

The examples of Cuba and China may be instructive in illuminating how basic changes in political systems influence the relationship of resource allocation, production and consumption, and population growth. Our imperfect observations of most of the developing world suggest the likelihood of substantial political and social change as the rule, rather than the exception. However difficult to capture in rigorous futuristic models, political change thus is a critical factor in developing a schemata for the future.

Even assuming that the ecologists have produced options that are based on all relevant factors, including considerations of political change, there is the critical question of who is to participate in choosing among the options. The ecologists present man and society with an entirely new agenda of advantages. Somebody has to decide how they are going to be distributed, to whom, in what quantity, and with what impact on whose life. Who, for example, is to tell the American suburbanite with two automobiles and a swimming pool that he must abandon this type of life style? And who is to tell the British coal miner living in a home without indoor plumbing and central heating that he should abandon hopes for these amenities because the British economy must continue to stagnate in the name of de-development? And who says "no" to the marginal population around Latin American cities dreaming of a better life, involving the consumption of more material amenities? But whoever participates in the choosing might well reflect on some critical questions raised by Rudolf Klein:

Do the anti-growth advocates assume that the existing social and economic structure of society will somehow be frozen—and that the present inequalities . . . will become happily accepted? Or do they assume a political system which insures that non-growth becomes a synonym for perpetuating existing inequalities . . . that economic stagnation can be reconciled with social change?[58]

The *Limits of Growth* team has attempted to anticipate this line of criticism with two arguments: First, "that the present patterns of population and capital growth are actually increasing the gap between the rich and the poor on a worldwide basis."[59] (They could have added that in developed nations the income gap between the lower and the upper classes has remained more or less static during the past few decades, despite an increase in the gross national product during the same period.) And, second, that in a no-growth society the lower classes, in being deprived of incremental benefits derived from economic growth, are bound to raise political demands for a more equitable share in the good things of life. More bluntly put, it is suggested that a no-growth society inevitably will generate class conflict centered on the issue of distributive justice.

However, this argument is persuasive only if it is assumed that in a no-growth society the lower classes will have sufficient opportunity effectively to make their demands. The assumption, however, is open to serious doubt because it is conditioned upon a redistribution of political power.

Within the international system, we are told by Ehrlich and the *Limits* team, a redistribution of income in favor of the masses in developing countries is essential to accommodate an ecologically and socially stable world. But there is no attempt to describe an international instrumentality that could be created realistically with sufficient power to compel or persuade developed nations—especially the United States and Soviet Union who are presently politically committed to increasing their gross national product—to relinquish their privileged economic and political positions.

But whatever its substantive merits or deficiencies, it is difficult to escape an elitist flavor in the ecological discourse. Scientists and intellectuals have analyzed society and ecology, and have concluded that certain restraints are necessary within both. They have formulated options and posed choices affecting mass publics who probably aspire to different conditions. But in their formulations there is no evidence of any real interchange between them and the mass publics whose world they would reconstruct. If the scientists systematically attempted to determine and calculate mass public preferences on these matters, the results are not evident as constraints on their remedies. Considering this critical gap, it is difficult to visualize mass acceptance of the *Limits* team's and Ehrlich's solutions under democratic conditions. Indeed, it could be reasonably argued that nothing short of a dictatorship of ecologists would do the job.

The ecologists could well be right in their prediction of ecological catastrophe for mankind in the foreseeable future unless fundamental socioeconomic and political changes are forthcoming. Certainly their predictions and supporting analysis cannot be discounted. They demand thorough and deep scrutiny. But, in the course of the scrutinizing, fundamental and complex political issues—issues which they ignore or gloss over—must also be analyzed and evaluated. This is of utmost importance. For it is not inconceivable that the political costs in terms of individual freedom required to achieve a "state of global equilibrium" is too high—even if ecological catastrophe is the alternative.

An Opportunity Forfeited

The Commission on Population Growth and the American Future provided a unique opportunity to confront and debate, in a highly visible public forum, the controversial issues raised in the ecological stream of the population policy discourse. Created by Act of Congress in 1970, and appointed by the President, the assignment of the 24-member commission was comprehensive:

to provide information and education to all levels of government in the United States and to our people regarding a broad range of problems associated with population growth and their implications for America's future.[60]

The range of issues raised in the ecological debate thus were relevant to the commission's mandate. But beyond recognizing that the ecological approach represented one of the key perspectives on problems of population growth, the commission resisted what could have been a fruitful encounter with its controversial substance. Instead, the commission's final report remains within familiar bounds and deals with issues in a familiar range.[61]

A significant indicator of the acceptability of the Commission's recommendations was their prompt endorsement by a group of prominent citizens under the leadership of the Population Crisis Committee, in a special supplement in the *New York Sunday Times.*[62] The Committee, which will be described in Chapter 4, is the principal lobbying arm of American industry and business in the population field. It is unlikely that the committee and its adherents would have endorsed recommendations that departed substantially from traditional approaches. The traditional family-planning context, which the Commission accepted, was more compatible with the committee's view of the world and the population problem, and clearly the committee found the commission's work consistent with this view.

It cannot be said that the commission avoided controversy. The recommendations on liberalization of abortion legislation and more widespread introduction of sex education in school curriculums addressed issues of high sensitivity. Their controversial character is reflected in President Nixon's prompt response to the commission's report, which was confined to a widely publicized unequivocal statement opposing both recommendations.[63]

But the issues of abortion and sex education are familiar ones in the traditional family-planning dialogue. They are included among the package of remedies to reduce fertility and to expand opportunities for individual choice in fertility decisions. Accordingly, the initial controversy generated by the commission's recommendations occurred within the familiar bounds of the traditional family-planning ideology. And, for the past two decades, this ideology has dominated the American dialogue on population growth.

Here, then, in the work of the commission we see a bias favoring the familiar and the traditional, and a resistance to venturing further afield, despite substantial justification for so doing. It is somewhat surprising that in a commission composed of a relatively large and diverse membership, only one commissioner, a Stanford law student, publicly expressed fundamental disagreement with the commission's final report.[64] Though some commissioners wrote dissenting statements on individual points, focused primarily on the issue of legalization of abortions, the commission emphasizes that there was "consensus of our members" on basic stance and recommendations. Because of this consensus, the commission expresses confidence that its recommendations "do indeed point the way in which this nation should move in solving its problems."[65]

At the outset of its report the commission expresses its major theme—that population stability must be sought with the object of substituting quality of life for quantity; quality of life that affords all human beings a "sense of their own dignity and worth, a sense of belonging and sharing, and the opportunity to develop their individual potentialities."[66] The commission's emphasis is upon the elimination of legal and social obstacles that prevent women from exercising their freedom of choice: freedom to control their life style and their bodies; freedom to control their fertility and freedom from the burden of bearing unwanted children.[67]

In grappling with the concept of "freedom of choice" the commissioners were aware that human "wants" and "preferences" are strongly influenced and shaped by the socialization process within which individuals are exposed by the traditions, customs, taboos, and expectations of their culture. Thus the commission recognized that both the informal and formal pronatalist institutions and customs required alteration if "rational" and "voluntary" choice was to prevail over custom of an out-moded tradition.[68] Side-stepping the question of what constitutes genuine cultural "neutrality" in this area—if indeed such neutrality can exist—the commission recommended, among its more radical proposals, affirmative legislation to provide minors under "appropriate settings" contraceptive information and other family planning services,[69] and liberalization of state abortion laws to permit a doctor to perform an abortion at a patient's request.[70]

Both recommendations were promptly rejected by President Nixon, who declared that "unrestricted abortion policies . . . (are) an unacceptable means of population control." He said that he preferred to rely on the good sense of the American people because he believed they would make "sound judgments, conducive both to public interest and personal family goals." The president expressed his belief "in the right of married couples to make these judgments for themselves."[71]

The basic commission position maintains that policies designed to slow population growth will significantly benefit everyone, irrespective of class, race, sex, or group. And in evaluating its recommendations, the commission claims they are consistent with the major and different perspectives from which population is viewed.[72] The commission maintains that population growth markedly contributes to every environmental problem: the ugliness, congestion, and squalor of cities, deterioration of countrysides, careless exploitation of energy and mineral resources, and the rapid growth in pollution of soil, air and water. Therefore it is claimed that a slower population growth rate will ease these problems, and, by "buying time," provide a greater opportunity to develop effective and democratic solutions to them.[73]

By adopting this approach the commission avoids the potentially explosive controversies involved in exploring interlocks among resources, affluence, population, and technology as a major cause of environmental deterioration. Escaping the heat of the ongoing ecological debate—and its political implications—the commission's approach to the population problem embodies a harmony of interest—an approach that is almost beyond politics, because there are no losers and all winners.

In addressing the growth/ecology problem, the commission maintains that a slower rate of population growth is congenial with higher output levels for the economy as a whole, a relationship which would cause higher per capita income, a reduction in poverty and pollution, and less drain on natural resources.[74] All sectors of society—business, labor, the poor—stand to gain as the rate of population growth approaches zero, and, as an added bonus, the rate of environmental deterioration declines.

All this would occur, it is claimed, since the rate of GNP growth required to support an increasing affluent society is less with a two-child (stable population) than with a three-child norm.[75]

The assumptions underlying this position would be questioned by the ecological school. They might argue that a commission concerned with quality of life would be disinclined, automatically, to assume that a "healthy economy" is one that generates continuing, albeit slower, economic growth. Some of the ecologists would say that the norm of acquisitiveness which pervades American life is the principal obstacle to higher quality life—not population growth. Indeed, one of the commissioners suggests that this malaise blinded the commission to other possibilities of what constitutes a "healthy economy."[76]

In framing the issue as the compatibility of slower population growth with a "healthy economy," the commission avoids the more basic problem: What rate of economic growth—if *any*—is compatible with a healthy ecology? By regarding economic growth as an imperative, the commission was able to ignore the contention of Ehrlich and the *Limits* team that a zero GNP growth-rate for the United States is among the essential requirements for the curtailment of environmental deterioration. And by avoiding the ecological argument, the commission could assure the American public that a slower population growth rate in no way will upset existing American standards of living.

The commission assumes that population size is a significant causal factor of environmental deterioration: "The total volume of pollutants in the United States responds . . . to the size of the national economy, which in turn depends heavily upon the size of the national population."[77] Thus, the smaller the population, the less pollution.

But ecologists might challenge this argument on two counts: (a) Slower population growth could indeed have a soothing effect on the environment, but will not economic growth, bolstered by a higher per capita income, counteract the effect? Ehrlich and others have emphasized that the impact of population on the environment must be measured not only by numbers of persons, but also by the level of affluence in a society.[78] Whatever the merit of this contention, the commission does not even mention it as a possible approach to the problem, much less examine its validity. (b) Technology is the principal cause of pollution as claimed by Commoner. Population size and the level of affluence could remain constant, but pollution could increase as a result of changing technology. Here again the commission did not dispose satisfactorily of a position that challenged its own.

Thus if either Ehrlich's or Commoner's position is correct, the commission's conclusion that "slower population growth offers us the difference between choice and necessity, between prudence and living dangerously"[79] would turn out to be fundamentally wrong.

When it tackles international dimensions, the commission similarly avoids confrontation of dissonant ecological positions. The commission believes "that, in its own interests, the United States should work positively and constructively with other countries and international organizations in analyzing and solving problems related to national resources and the environment in the world."[80]

But the commission does not respond to Ehrlich's widely-discussed charge that a nation which is the world's largest consumer of non-renewable resources and the greatest offender of the world's ecology cannot justify any further economic expansion and increased affluence.

This global challenge was articulated by Maurice F. Strong at the Conference on Human Environment: " 'No growth' is not a viable policy for any society today. . . . Indeed, people must have access to more, not fewer, opportunities to express their creative drive. But these can only be provided with a total system in which man's activities are in dynamic harmony with the natural order." To achieve this condition, he added, "We must rethink our concepts of the basic purposes of growth. Surely we must see it in terms of enriching the lives and enlarging the *opportunities of all mankind*. And if this is so, it follows that it is the more wealthy society—the privileged minority of mankind—which *will have to make the most profound and even revolutionary, changes in attitudes and values*."[81]

Dealing with Strong's formulation would have required the abandonment of a nonpolitical "within system" approach to the population problem. The commission apparently was not prepared to move this far. Because of its reluctance to broaden its outlook beyond a harmony-of-interest context, the commission relied heavily upon the traditional family-planning approach as the framework within which to operate.

Accordingly, among numerous recommendations those regarding contraceptive technology are accorded top priority. In the commission's words, it "recommends that this nation give the *highest priority* to research in reproductive biology and to research for improved methods by which individuals can control their own fertility."[82] In this connection it is notable that only the recommendations on birth control technology and family planning carry specific dollar figures.[83]

In dealing with environmental problems the commission emphasizes a formula involving the application of technology, harnessed to "private market forces,"[84] to successfully combat environmental deterioration. Although it recognizes that appropriate public "institutional and legal underpinnings" are necessary if private industry is to fulfill this task, the commission is quick to add that "institutional arrangements for channeling private interests" must be achieved "without undue government regulations."[85]

In contrast to the specificity of the commission's recommendations on contraceptive technology and family planning the proposals concerning the maldistribution of urban population are less precise. Although it pulls no punches in condemning widespread institutional racism in America, and urges corrective measures, the related commission recommendations for action are general in nature. For example, on the key problem of racial polarization in urban areas, the commission recommends "vigorous and concerted steps to promote free choice of housing within metropolitan areas."[86] This is indeed forceful language, but the "concerted steps" that the commission suggests are nebulous. For example, it proposes that the federal government take a more active role to guarantee local compliance with housing laws, and suggests that new institutions might be established to assist ethnic and racial minorities in finding suburban housing.[87]

On this pressing problem for many Americans, the commission states:

Fuller and more refined goals, policies, and strategies must be generated over time as we learn—through experimentation with alternative measures, through further research, and, through continuous monitoring of trends—how best to influence the pattern that population redistribution takes.[88]

Considering the unique opportunity to propose some specific initiatives for overcoming known pathologies in the distribution of American population, the Commission call for more study hardly meets the expectations of those who are known to be suffering from maldistribution.

Whatever the evaluation of the commission's work, there is cause for concern because it resists dealing with the broad range of issues opened by the ecological debate, and the political and economic implications that flow from these issues. An opportunity has been forfeited to confront the American public with some hard realities about the limited rewards to be realized from curbing population growth. In steering clear of the ecological debate, the report depicts a relatively painless course of action in which all will stand to benefit, in which neither the existing power structure nor basic values would be challenged, and in which the quality of life would improve, while time could be bought to develop solutions to environmental problems in a rational and orderly manner. Underlying this gloss of rationality are unexplained major premises and an argument tailored to avoid difficult issues—issues which raise the spectre that fundamental changes in American values and power relationships may be necessary to achieve ecological well-being. This is provocative and complex political subject matter.

We have suggested that this range of issues now comprises the most important ingredient for a dialogue about population policy in the United States. Yet we have found that the latest and most visible enterprise in American population policy-making—The Commission on Population Growth and the American Future—has not dealt with them. Instead the commission has consciously or unconsciously engaged in nondecision-making by constructing a policy making agenda within a limited and familiar range, and by simultaneously limiting the scope of controversy that might enlarge it.

3

Beyond Family Planning

Two Forms of Non-Decision-Making

The limitations imposed on the scope of controversy in the American population policy discourse, whether consciously or unconsciously, are illustrated more specifically by two examples of non-decision-making that have emerged from within the Population Coalition.

It was suggested earlier that there are two forms of non-decision-making. The first form, which is the most indirect, is a decision which has the effect of strengthening and sustaining the *mobilization of bias*; i.e., that reinforces the established way of looking at things. By achieving this objective, the ongoing system becomes less vulnerable to attack by its critics. For example, pronouncements extolling the glories of free enterprise tend to render the existing system less vulnerable to ideological competition.

The second and more direct type of non-decision-making is one in which a component or components of *mobilization of bias* are utilized as instrumentalities to discredit emerging hostile positions. If such an act prevents an issue from entering the public arena, it may be said to be a successful non-decision. For example, a demand or position may be denied legitimacy by asserting that it is socialistic, illegal, or in violation of an established procedure, rule, or existing value.

During recent years, two episodes within the population-policy discourse illustrated these forms of non-decision-making. These episodes are significant, because of their probable effect on the discourse and because they emanated from notable sources in the population field—one an individual and the other a group.

A Form of Non-Decision-Making

"Beyond Family Planning," a well-known article by Bernard Berelson, President of the Population Council, is a subtle but forceful illustration of the first form of non-decision-making.[1] The author's declared purpose in writing the article is to encourage further consideration of alternative proposals that extend beyond the currently-accepted boundaries of the family-planning strategy. Berelson concludes his thoughtful study by stating that "it is natural and desirable that counter positions should be put forward and reviewed."[2]

The article reflects a comprehensive inventory of proposals for influencing population growth that venture beyond the traditional family-planning formulations. But the encouragement to broaden the dialogue by considering the alternatives seriously appears equivocal in light of the treatment they receive in the article. The proposals are examined on the basis of a set of limited criteria which themselves appear to be products of a normative bias favoring the family-planning ideology. The criteria themselves, and their underlying norms, are not challenged. Thus, limitations determined by these norms are imposed upon the broadened discourse. In non-decision-making terminology, Berelson has employed values congenial to the dominant position in the population-policy discourse in order to set boundaries on its expansion. And, as a result, family-planning goals are reinforced, while the emergence of challenges to these goals is discouraged.

Berelson sets forth six criteria by which to evaluate "beyond family-planning" proposals: (1) scientific/medical/technological readiness, (2) political viability, (3) administrative feasibility, (4) economic capability, (5) moral/ethical/philosophical acceptability, and (6) presumed effectiveness.[3]

All the criteria appear to be rooted in the *status quo*; that is to say, in the relevant conditions as we know them today. For example, the first criterion—scientific/medical/technological readiness—is related directly to a readiness to produce and deliver contraceptive services. Thus the criterion accepts the salience of contraceptive services as established in the family-planning ideology. The possibility of a changed state of readiness, one induced by a different *status quo*, and one that might involve a lesser salience for contraceptive technology, is excluded as a likely standard for evaluation.

Under the second criterion, political viability, Berelson evaluates proposed programs in terms of their likelihood of giving acceptance by *existing* governments, and their ability to "fix within the framework of *existing* values, elite or mass, and preferably both . . . " (Emphasis ours.) On the basis of his assumption that underdeveloped societies will remain politically and socially static during the next decade or so, the family-planning approach is likely to win the day. For, as he makes clear in his introductory remarks, one of the major strengths of this approach is that it has received wide political acceptance throughout the underdeveloped world.[4] However, the possible demographic impact of substantial social and political change in a single developing country, i.e., Cuba, suggests that Berelson's treatment of this dimension may be unduly confined in resting upon the assumption of a static political system.[5]

The notion of political acceptability could well be extended beyond speculation exclusively on the adoption of antinatalist proposals by existing governments. It might also include speculation about how political change might change the political acceptability of policy options capable of influencing population growth rates, and the differential impact on the rates of this revised set of options.

If population specialists adopted this broader approach, research interest could, perhaps, be generated to include studies on changing political and social structures—both in the United States and abroad—and their relationships to changing population policies and related socialization patterns. However, if these kinds of issues continue to be overshadowed by concentration on contraceptive technology and its delivery within existing societies, traditional family-planning research could persist in dominating the field.

The same kind of criticism can be leveled at Berelson's interpretation of the remaining criteria. His discussion of each criterion assumes the maintenance of the existing political structure. For example, in his analysis of administrative feasibility, he states, "Several proposals assume administrable workability of a complicated scheme in a country that cannot *now* collect its own vital statistics in a reliable manner."[6] (Emphasis ours.) Under the heading, "Economic Capability," he asks two questions: "Is the program worthwhile when measured against the criterion of economic return? And can it be afforded from *present* budgets, even if worthwhile?"[7] (Emphasis ours.)

Under the key criterion of moral/ethical/philosophical acceptability, he again assumes the maintenance of the *status quo*. He addresses himself to the question, "Is the proposal considered right and proper—by the target population, government officials, professional or intellectual elites, and the outside agencies committed to assistance?"[8]

What he does not consider is that the reaction of a target population under one set of socioeconomic and political conditions may be quite different from under another set.[9]

The attitude of Chinese women to childbearing is a case in point. In sharp contrast to their prenatal behavior in the recent past, reports from China suggest that now they apparently do not regard large families as a personally desirable goal.[10] Because of their changed mores and social behavior, it is probable that their attitude about what constitutes a constraint or support of their freedom—including their "right" to procreate—will also have changed. If the subject of moral acceptability is analyzed within the context of possible social change, then the problem is not solely one of adjusting a program to the present values of a people; it also entails the question of what socioecomonic and political changes are necessary to move societal values toward an effective antinatalist policy, if such is the desired objective.

The political significance of the article is its confinement to the *status quo*, in which family planning cannot help but score exceptionally high in contrast to proposals that would necessitate broad changes in social and political institutions.

The "beyond family-planning" remedies that Berelson proposes as ripe for adoption do not conflict with the ingredients of ongoing family-planning programs and the philosophy underlying them. They include "institutionalization of maternal care, population study in the schools, the TV satellite system for information purposes, a better contraceptive technology, perhaps even liberalization of abortion in some settings. . ."[11] All of these proposals supplement, augment, and otherwise support the traditional family-planning approach.

Deliberate or not, Berelson's analysis is an example of non-decision-making in the population policy field. It sustains and strengthens, subtly yet forcefully, the dominant family-planning philosophy while refuting challenging positions. The consequence could be to discourage consideration and review of proposals beyond family planning that are not adaptable to existing social structures in many countries.

Whatever the reason, it is important to note that later, in a more recent article, Berelson welcomes fresh and new ideas comparing population policy-making. He emphasizes that "Population policy is a policy of means, not ends. . . . The consideration of such ends involves ethical questions, not technical or scientific ones."[12] This position represents a significant departure from the traditional *status quo* bias of the family-planning strategy. The question now is whether Berelson will succeed in developing this line of reasoning, and whether it will actually carry him beyond family planning.

Another Non-Decision

The second form of non-decision-making is illustrated by a debate in the pages of *Science* In an article critical of family planning, Kingsley Davis argues that family planning fails to confront the real problem: that women not only bear "too many" children, but they also actually want to have too many children. He claims that merely providing contraceptive education and devices will not halt undesirable population growth, and that family planning will not produce population control.[13]

While Davis agreed with family-planning advocates that population control should occur within a context of voluntarism, he loaded the context within which individual choice is exercised. He suggests that our "social structure must be changed," to suppress the desire of all segments of the female population for more than three children. He proposed that antinatalist attitudes be fostered, that women be given access to a wider variety of roles, and that marriages be delayed. He criticizes the attitude of many population specialists, charging that they seem frightened of the desirable goal of zero population growth.

A reply to Davis' critique was forthcoming from his colleagues. In a letter published in *Science*, the Committee on Population of the National Academy of Sciences stated:

A zero rate of population growth may be essential in the long run, but as a goal within the time horizon of current policy it has *little support* in either the developing or the developed world, certainly not among governments. Before any action in this direction is taken, it will be necessary to develop some *consensus* in support of the goal itself. . . . Programs of social change must operate within the framework of *existing values* and few governments are yet prepared to adopt stringent economic or social means to bring down birth rates.[14] (Emphasis ours.)

Admittedly a political strategy built upon consensus cannot be rejected out of hand. It appears somewhat unrealistic, however, to believe that a political consensus can be developed in support of a goal that might require substantial changes in the structures, norms, and power relationships in societies. Because of its untenable position on this issue, the committee appears to have attempted to use its prestige and influence to reject substantive recommendations that it could not or did not wish to consider on their merits. Davis, himself an Academy member, noted in a letter of reply that the committee is "funded by the Population Council, foremost advocate of family planning for population control," in an attempt "to bring the Academy's prestige to the support of family planning."[15]

The motivation of the committee aside, its letter raises a serious ethical question; namely, the propriety of a prestigious scientific committee discouraging, for other than substantive reasons, further debate—as well as further research and investigation—on an important and unresolved issue. The letter, signed by leading authorities in the population field and under the aegis of the top scientific organization in the country, could have no other effect. The scientists were clearly attempting to exercise power by the non-decision-making route, and probably successfully. For, in proclaiming that a zero population growth objective must await a consensus, it is likely that the committee's letter had the effect of strengthening the existing consensus for family planning.

Davis himself, in his rebuttal missive, observed that he was being ignored, not on the effectiveness of his proposal, but, instead, on the grounds of its acceptability. Not allowing their "minds to break out of the tyranny of what *is*, to think effectively of what *can be*," the Academy committee chose to totally escape even "consideration of the painful social and economic changes necessary to achieve fertility control."[16]

Besides having a "chilling effect" on future debate and research on this issue within the scientific community, the letter also could have the effect of narrowing the exposure of policy-makers to relevant considerations and options in their deliberations and formulation of public policy. It is assumed that by the nature of policy processes, bureaucratic heads and political elites engage in non-decision-making. However, it is contrary to the spirit of scientific inquiry, which is their principal professional task, for scholars to exercise power in this way. The committee members, reflecting normative preferences, refused to consider the possibility that social change can become a viable means to achieve population-limitation goals. In so doing, they failed to recognize that existing values may be a major obstacle to solving a problem about which they expressed concern.

A Caveat

Had the Davis position been accepted and placed on the discussion agenda, it would have sharpened the population discourse by raising two issues of both demographic and political salience: (1) the impact of structural change on fertility behavior; (2) the conditions for communal intervention in individual fertility behavior.

There is evidence in the United States and elsewhere that structural change is a potentially powerful agent in influencing fertility behavior. People enjoying better lives and greater opportunities tend to regulate and reduce their fertility performance independently. But the critical question is, Who determines the structural change—its quality, timing, and impact?

The implicit thrust of Davis' position is that the United States, for example, were it sufficiently bold, could contribute significantly toward achieving population stability in Latin America by fostering social revolution in this area. From what we know of the Cuban experience, such strategy could well contribute to a resolution of the population growth problem in this hemisphere. But who is to say that the United States should become the Platonic guardian for millions of Latin Americans? Moreover—and, also from a democratic perspective—are we prepared to foster a crop of dictatorships, albeit of a left variety, after years of liberal cant about the evils of gunboat diplomacy?

The same kind of questions arise when considering Davis' position as it might affect American society. It is not inconceivable, for example, that the Population Coalition could be persuaded that social change in the United States is a necessary condition in order to secure a stable population. Might not the adoption of this position by such an elite alliance lead to the establishment of a limited set of conditions and boundaries wihin which the American public would be permitted to make choices? This we see as the implication, although undoubtedly an unintended one, of Davis' argument.

Structural decisions by the powerful, designed to influence the fertility performance of the powerless, might well promote inequitable policies. In Jaffe's words:

... most of the social and economic constraints . . . would not fall equally on all Americans in a society as stratified as ours. Many of them . . . would penalize children already born, rather than deter the conception of additional ones . . . once the idea is legitimated that family-size decisions, should be directly influenced by society rather than left up to the parents themselves, the concept would be seized upon for a reinvigorated campaign of compulsion aimed at the most powerless people in the United States—the poor, the welfare recipients, and the minorities.[17]

We would argue that the conditions of society—how people live and are permitted to live—are the principal determinants of fertility behavior, and thus the Davis position is central to any discourse on population policy. At the same time, we would maintain that the processes by which the conditions of society are established is equally salient to a discourse on population or any other sort of policy.

These are some of the significant issues that the Davis position, however evaluated, opens up. To attempt, by whatever techniques, to prevent these issues from being fully debated and aired is to perpetuate the traditional task-oriented and technological orientation of the population-growth discourse.

Thus, the most damaging effect of non-decision-making exercised at the scholarly level is that .it prevents policy-makers from becoming aware of all possible alternatives. Policy-makers can hardly formulate enlightened public policy if their exposure is only to the orthodox and safe. The impact of this limited discourse to which the specialists and scientists have been major contributors is exemplified in the following report from AID (the largest governmental distributor of funds for population programs):

Because the extent of availability of family-planning information and means is not usually a dominant determinant in the complex of forces influencing representative behavior, *no definitive studies nor final judgments of additional measures which may ultimately be needed to achieve a desired rate of population growth can be made in advance of the full extension of family-planning services.*[18] (Emphasis ours.)

**Part II:
The Structure of Policy
Formulation**

4   The Anatomy of a Coalition

An Emerging Concern

During the postwar decade a small group of prescient American scientists became increasingly aware that rapidly growing populations in developing countries constituted a major obstacle to their development and critically threatened their ability to feed themselves. It was this recognition that provided the incentives, particularly in the intellectual and scientific communities, to explore systematically the dimensions of the problem. Thus, in 1948 the Rockefeller Foundation, a pioneer in supporting such enterprises, sponsored a survey in five Far Eastern countries by a group of demographers and health specialists who reported that "those of the reduction of human fertility are at once most difficult and important" among the problems of human welfare in the Far East.[1]

As for the United States itself, population concerns were confined to microcosmic matters, such as the ability of growing families to take care of themselves and, specifically, care for the well-being of individual mothers and children. This concern for individual welfare had been the inspiration for the Planned Parenthood movement in the United States during the previous five decades.

Created and nurtured by Margaret Sanger, a pioneer of women's lib, the Planned Parenthood movement was built on a nationwide network of private local affiliates whose single objective was the provision of birth control information and materials to (mostly poor)[2] females in need. Prior to 1950 the Planned Parenthood Federation of America was the only group in the public or private sector actively promoting birth control. The subject of fertility regulation was still a political taboo in the public sector, and so government agencies were inactive in the field.

Prewar population interests in the academic community took the form of scattered research enterprises on population and fertility problems. As early as 1922, the Scripps Foundation for Research in Population Problems was established at Miami University, in Ohio. In 1928 the Milbank Memorial Fund initiated its program of support for fertility research. In 1929 the Population Preference Bureau was established to gather, analyze, and disseminate information on population subjects. The first Rockefeller Foundation grant in the population field was made to the Social Science Research Council in 1934 for a study of population distribution. And in 1936, the Office of Population

Research was established at Princeton University, much of the funding coming from the Rockefeller Foundation. An Institute of Population Research was set up at Louisiana State University in 1938. And in 1948 an Office of Population Research was created in the Sociology Department of the University of Washington.[3]

The Intellectual Core

The rapid development of a core of knowledge emerged as the priority objective of a small but growing group of individuals and institutions who were becoming concerned about population growth. The priority for knowing something before doing something was a fortunate condition for all concerned, because the process is frequently reversed in American policy-making. However, because government intervention in population growth still was a sensitive political issue, the political pressures that might otherwise demand immediate results, whatever the state of knowledge, were absent, at least for the time being.

Accordingly, scientists and intellectuals in the universities, supported initially by their peers in the foundations, could proceed with the task of enlarging their knowledge and capacities, and independently determine how their activities might best be utilized for policy-making purposes. Perhaps because they were able to take the initiative at this early stage, the scientists and intellectuals, and the institutions in which they were based, were able to establish a preeminent position in the policy-making process.

A conference on population problems held at Williamsburg, Virginia in June, 1952 was the major catalyst for creation of an expanded intellectual core. Convened at the initiative of John D. Rockefeller 3rd, the meeting was sponsored by the National Academy of Sciences. The conference objectives were posed in global terms:

Conference on Population Problems

1. The purpose of the conference is to consider available facts and conflicting views about the effects of population growth on human welfare, to the end that it may be possible to reach conclusions stimulating thought and, perhaps, action.

Some believe that unless measures to reduce the birth rate in several areas are quickly and successfully applied, the rapid growth of world population in relation to resources may have catastrophic results. Others think that the probable development of technology and progress in the application of technology will soon make possible a satisfactory level of living for the entire human race, and that efforts need be directed only to the increase of production throughout the world. Many intermediate points of view are also held.

2. The aim of the conference is to obtain the greatest possible agreement among the participants concerning the following questions:

(a) Is rapid population growth in the near future likely to lead to grave difficulties in the nonindustrial countries of the world, or for the world as a whole?

(b) If so, what, if any, elements in the situation should be influenced by planned action; e.g., should attempts be made to reduce the birth rate, or to speed the movement to the cities, or to speed rural development, etc.?

(c) What practical steps are likely to produce the desired changes?[4]

The Williamsburg meeting was attended by thirty participants, most of whom were physical and social scientists from universities throughout the United States. In addition, there were representatives of the Rockefeller Foundation, individuals from the federal government, who attended in their private capacities, and staff members of the Planned Parenthood Federation.

The one specific action taken by the Williamsburg Conference was a resolution to create a temporary committee to plan the establishment of a permanent international council to carry on the aims and purposes of the conference, with emphasis upon developing societies.

Within a historical perspective it is noteworthy that the Williamsburg Conference recommended the establishment of a new body to "quarterback" intellectual expansion in population affairs. Considering existing political sensitivities, this initiative could not yet be taken by a public agency. However, given their interests, autonomy, and independent position, it was a legitimate role for the largest private foundations in the United States—Rockefeller and Ford, both of which were financing intellectual development in other fields. But the same sensitivities about intervention in population matters which discouraged initiatives by the federal government, for the time being, restricted an open role by the foundations. Accordingly, John D. Rockefeller 3rd, Chairman of the Rockefeller Foundation Board, initiated the Williamsburg meeting to seek an alternate base for action in an area he considered critical. Through this new vehicle, the foundations could encourage and initiate actions they considered necessary, but could not take directly.

The determination of Rockefeller, buttressed by the consensus expressed at Williamsburg, resulted in the formation of The Population Council in the fall of 1952. This council was funded with start-up capital from the Rockefeller family, and two years later that funding was augmented by generous grants from the Rockefeller Foundation and the Ford Foundation.

Since its formation, the Council, in fact, has assumed a leadership role in the population field both domestically and internationally, primarily by supporting the development of research and teaching institutions, and training of individuals who work in them. The major objective of the Council program has been the production and dissemination of knowledge of the causes and consequences of population change. On the action side, the Council has been active in an energetic program of contraceptive research, contraceptive product development, and deployment of family-planning programs in developing countries.

To mount these efforts The Population Council gathered an eminent group of medical and social scientists as staff members and consultants. They developed the strategies, and programmed the growing levels of financing from private individuals and foundations, and, more recently, from the federal government. By 1970, The Population Council had disposed of nearly $90 million.[5]

The activities initiated by the Council and its supporters produced a significant expansion in the intellectual sector of the population field. This expansion evolved principally in the American university system, through the creation of teaching and research activities supported by grants, contracts, and fellowships, first originating from The Population Council as a conduit, then directly from the Rockefeller and Ford Foundations, and by the mid-60s from the federal government. These activities were based primarily in schools of medicine and public health, departments of sociology and demography, and in newly-created population centers.

In levels of activities and funding, the major American population centers emerged at the Rockefeller University, which houses The Population Council's intramural unit for research in reproductive physiology; the University of North Carolina; the University of Michigan; Tulane University; Harvard University; Johns Hopkins University; the University of Hawaii; Columbia University; and the University of California. Smaller, but nonetheless important programs were activated at Georgetown, Texas, Brown, Pittsburgh, Wisconsin, Cornell, Duke, and Notre Dame. A major training-and-research program in reproductive physiology was established at the Worcester Foundation for Experimental Biology.

By 1971 the Population Association of America was able to report the existence of population studies programs at fifty-one American universities.[6] This inventory was confined to programs in anthropology, demography, public health, and sociology. In addition to these primarily social-science programs, a growing number and variety of teaching and research enterprises in reproductive physiology, and related biomedical fields, were launched in American medical schools.[7]

The Private Activists

Parallel with the efforts of John D. Rockefeller 3rd on behalf of the intellectual sector, were the efforts of Hugh Moore in the private sector. From the platform of a family foundation, the Hugh Moore Fund, Moore first set out to create public awareness and action in the early fifties by supporting publication of a pamphlet called "The Population Bomb," which reflected some of Moore's anxieties:

Today the population bomb threatens to create an explosion as disruptive and dangerous as the explosion of the atom, and with as much influence on prospects for progress or disaster, war or peace. . .[8]

The impact of "The Population Bomb" was described in an account of Moore's activities:

The booklet's whiplash phraseology stung a dormant public, and its relentless parade of facts and figures—about booming birth rates, looming famines, zooming taxes, all likely to breed war—made uncomfortable but compelling reading.[9]

On this basis Moore embarked upon a campaign to mobilize public opinion, particularly that of prominent American citizens, in an organized effort for direct political action to control population growth. His technique was described in the same account of his activities:

Now he poured four decades of management and merchandising skills into the population movement with the same determination he had employed when, a few months out of Harvard, he peddled a bizarre idea—the paper cup.[10]

During ensuing years, the enterprise that Moore started in the early 1950s was reflected in a series of full-page newspaper advertisements that appeared periodically in the *New York Times* and other leading American newspapers (see Figure 4-1—Time Bomb Ad). These advertisements, which portrayed the theme expressed in "The Population Bomb," were signed by a group of prominent Americans from public life, business, industry, the professions, and the academic world.

In 1965, Moore and his associates created a permanent lobbying group in Washington called The Population Crisis Committee, which has developed into an energetic and highly visible spokesman for the interests it represents. The major figure in the Population Crisis Committee has been a prominent American banker and public servant, General William H. Draper Jr., the author of a 1959 report on foreign aid, which first recommended support for fertility-reduction programs in developing countries.

The makeup of the Population Crisis Committee reflected Moore's determination to enlist prominent and influential Americans in the cause. The committee's membership reflects a profile that might well provide an archetype of C. Wright Mills' concept of an American power elite. It is an impressive array of American notabilia—officers of major corporations, retired ambassadors and generals, prominent academic figures, members of leading law firms, and both active and retired government officials.[11]

Notably absent in the committee's membership are blacks and the poor, the public constituency that is the target of subsidized family-planning services in the United States. Thus, considering its predominance within the business/industry membership, the Population Crisis Committee can be regarded as a spokesman for American corporate enterprise.

Whereas the Population Crisis Committee reflects a limited strata in American society, the other major lobbying group in the population field attempts to involve a much more broadly-based constituency. Thus, Zero Population

48

THE NEW YORK TIMES

Dear President Nixon:
The underlying problem facing your administration will not be war, riots or crime but the population bomb

In the four year term of office to which you have been elected there will be *ten million more* Americans—most of them living in our already over-crowded cities.

And there will be *three hundred million more* people in the world at the present rate of increase—most of them without enough to eat.

Fourteen million people will die of starvation during your term of office unless the present death rate of ten thousand a day is reduced. (America cannot feed the world, as we have found after shipping $15 billion worth of food abroad in recent years.)

There were 2½ billion people in the world in 1953. Today only 15 years later there are *one billion more!* This basic problem, Mr. President, bears directly or indirectly on most of the problems you will have to deal with during your Administration.

To check the population explosion —both in this country and abroad— you must seek appropriations many times larger than those heretofore allocated for birth control by your Govern-ment. Surely a nation which approves $1½ billion to develop a new military airplane can afford to devote a comparable sum to the solution of the most urgent problem of the human race!

For there is little doubt that unless population is brought under control *at an early date* the resulting social tensions and misery will inevitably lead to chaos and strife—to revolutions and wars which may make our present experience in Vietnam minor by comparison.

Nothing less than the survival of civilization is in the balance.

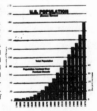

CAMPAIGN TO CHECK THE POPULATION EXPLOSION
60 EAST 42nd STREET, NEW YORK, NEW YORK 10017
EMERSON FOOTE, CHAIRMAN

Figure 4-1. Perspective for Population Policy-making

Growth, which was organized in 1969, has evolved into the largest private-interest group concerned with population matters. Claiming a membership of 35,000 members and 330 chapters throughout the United States, ZPG was inspired by the population/environment nexus developed and popularized by Paul Ehrlich, its honorary president. Although ZPG extends into the communities, it is principally an organization for the young, with its major constituency based largely in the faculties and student bodies of American universities.[1][2]

Although the central purpose of the third major citizen's group, historically, has been the provision of contraceptive services to individuals in need, the Planned Parenthood Federation of America during recent years has added communication, information, and programmatic functions to its traditional service role. Planned Parenthood is in a favorable position to do so. The organization is made up of a nationwide network of Planned Parenthood affiliates, comprising 183 local boards in thirty-eight states, with an average of thirty persons on each board. This network, involving a national membership of approximately 6,000, has been characterized as a "junior league-type" organization.[1][3]

With the expansion of population interest and activities in the United States during the middle sixties, Planned Parenthood created a new unit—the Center for Family Planning Program Development—to provide technical assistance for family-planning programs in the United States. In addition, a quarterly publication, "Family Planning Perspectives," was initiated to report on scientific and programmatic developments in the family-planning field. Also, periodic reports on the status of government activity in the population/family-planning field are issued by Planned Parenthood's Washington office. Although it engages in no overt lobbying activities, the Washington office of Planned Parenthood has been credited with directing the successful legislative strategy that resulted in passage of the "Tyding's Bill" in 1969, and increasingly has assumed a leading role in government relations on behalf of population/family-planning interests.

A Government Commitment

By the early 1960s the emergence of a more permissive political climate allowed the federal government to assume an active and direct role in the population field. In no small measure the change in Washington climate resulted from the convergence of intellectual activities in the universities and political activities from within the private citizen's groups. Researchers were verifying that population growth indeed was a major social and economic problem, and they were discovering dramatic new means to control fertility. And, the private activists were creating channels to reach political leaders, an expanding spectrum of influential citizens, and the public.

It is notable that the U.S. government's initial entry into the population field was prompted by anxieties about the harmful effects of population growth in developing countries. These concerns were being expressed most directly in the Hugh Moore-group advertisements.

For there is little doubt that unless population is brought under control *at an early date* the resulting social tensions and misery will inevitably lead to chaos and strife–to revolutions and wars which may make our present experience in Vietnam minor by comparison.[14]

By the end of the decade of the fifties, there was little to show in the way of economic and social progress as a result of substantial injections of American foreign aid. A variety of formulas designed to achieve instant development were not working. The search for more effective developmental approaches and for flaws in the ongoing programs became a priority for American development planning. In 1959 President Eisenhower created another committee, in a long series of foreign aid evaluations, to study the Military Assistance Program headed by General William H. Draper, Jr. As a result of its examinations of developing countries receiving military assistance, the Draper Committee concluded that rapid population growth was a major obstacle to development, and recommended early channeling of foreign aid into population control programs.[15] President Eisenhower promptly rejected the idea as an improper area for government intervention. Nonetheless, the Draper Report established the control of rapid population growth as a legitimate item on the agenda of American foreign aid.

The Kennedy Administration took the first cautious steps in addressing the issue that Draper had posed four years earlier. In 1963 President Kennedy formally agreed to make available the results of American fertility research through the United Nations.[16]

At the outset of his first full term in 1965, President Johnson opened the door wider by announcing his State of the Union Message, "I will seek new ways to use our knowledge to help deal with the explosion in world population."[17] At the same time, there was an opening on the domestic side in legitimitizing the provision of federal support for unmet needs in family-planning information and services in the United States. Obviously with top-level approval, the Surgeon General issued a memorandum stating, "The Public Health Service encourages the application of its resources to the important health-related problems in the population field."[18]

So, as the Williamsburg Conference in 1952 represented a watershed in the intellectual sector, so did these two Johnson Administration decisions of early 1965 comprise a comparable transition for the public sector. For the balance of the decade, events followed in rapid order as the government commitment became institutionalized, with new organizations, programs, and funding aimed at influencing both domestic and international fertility and population-growth problems. The major role on the international scene was assigned to the Agency for International Development within which a Population Office was created in 1966. Between fiscal years 1966 and 1971, authorizations for population activities in AID programs rose from annual rates of $10 to $125 million dollars a year.[19] In 1967, a position of Special Assistant to the Secretary of State for Population Matters was created in the State Department.

To administer research programs on the domestic side, a Center for Population Research was created in the National Institute of Child Health and Human Development (NICHD) in 1966. And to administer the funding of family-planning services, a Center for Family Planning Services was established in Health Services and Mental Health Administration Program (HSMHA) in 1969. To coordinate both the research and service arms of federal domestic programs in the Department of Health, Education and Welfare, a position of Deputy Assistant Secretary for Population Affairs was created in the HEW hierarchy in 1968.

The Office of Economic Opportunity was authorized in 1966 to include family-planning services as an ingredient in its community action programs, and a population unit was established in OEO's Office of Health Affairs to administer these activities.

As population units were set up in agencies of the government, scientific advisory units, composed of outside experts (mostly from universities), were created within them. Thus, in the Center for Population Research a number of Research Advisory Panels were established to evaluate research proposals submitted to the Center. A Population Advisory Group was created within the Agency for International Development to advise on overall agency strategy in population programs. And, in The National Academy of Sciences, a group of specialists was organized to study the consequences of population change during 1955 and 1966.[20]

In addition to these formally established groups, population specialists from outside the government frequently were invited to perform ad-hoc consultative assignments. One of the most significant of these enterprises was the joint effort of Oscar Harkavy of the Ford Foundation, Frederick Jaffe of Planned Parenthood/World Population, and Samuel Wishik of Columbia University, who collaborated in a study of how the Department of Health, Education and Welfare should discharge the responsibilities it had assumed in the population and family-planning fields.[21]

The first surge of activity at the federal level culminated in 1968 with the appointment by President Johnson of a President's Committee on Population and Family Planning. This committee brought together a group of recognized specialists, principally from the foundations, universities, and government agencies, to make specific recommendations on the federal government's role in the population field. One recommendation was for the establishment of a public commission to study the causes and consequences of population growth in the United States. This objective was achieved by Congressional authorization of a

Commission on Population Growth and the American Future, established in 1970. Unlike the committee set up by President Johnson, the commission appointed in 1970 by President Nixon contained, in addition to a core of population specialists, some non-expert representation from various sectors of the American public.

It could be said that formal Congressional recognition of the population issue was symbolized by the initiation of hearings on population growth in a Senate Government Operation Sub-Committee chaired by Senator Gruening in 1965. Although they began in a relatively obscure corner of the Senate structure, the marathon Gruening Committee hearings, which lasted from 1965 to 1968, provided an opportunity for the systematic airing of prevailing knowledge and opinions on the population growth problem.[22] Doing this in a Congressional forum endowed the issue with a visibility and legitimacy that it heretofore had not acquired.

Proceedings on Capitol Hill are an accurate reflector of the priorities within the attention span of the American public. Sometimes Congressional activities take the form of initiatives that move slightly ahead of public concerns, and at other times Congressional activity is positioned slightly in their wake. But, whether in front or behind, Congressional activity is never too far away from the main body of public concern. Thus, the activity of the Ninety-first Congress (1969-1971) in the population field is noteworthy, because by comparison to years past, it represented a fresh surge of interest. Two pieces of population legislation were enacted—The Family Planning Services and Population Research Act of 1970 (Public Law 91-572), and an Act to Establish a Commission of Population Growth and the American Future (Public Law 91-213). Additional legislation authorized and appropriated increased levels of funding for domestic and overseas population and family-planning activities. In addition to legislation actually passed, there were four sets of public hearings which explored various aspects of the population issue.[23]

Beyond legislation enacted and the hearings, a number of legislative proposals in the population area were introduced in both houses. Though they were neither enacted nor the subject of formal hearings, a total of thirty-four bills on population matters were introduced in the House and Senate. These proposals were sponsored by a total of thirty Senators and thirty-eight Representatives. They spanned the range of possible legislative actions in the population field—including statements of position, creation of commissions and conferences, manipulation of the tax and tariff structures, legislative and executive branch reorganization, authorizations and limitations on expenditures and Congressional investigations.[24]

In addition to the sixty-eight members of Congress involved in the sponsorship of these proposals, there were thirty-three Senate sponsors and 126 House sponsors of the Tyding's Bill and Population Commission legislation that actually was enacted. Thus, population had penetrated the legislative attention span of a significant portion of the membership in Congress.

Networks and Interlocks

By 1970, with the government fully committed in the population field to the extent of openly talking about the problems, and being willing to provide large amounts of money and the authority to do something about them, the last of the interested institutions had taken its place in an American Population Coalition. We have identified four types of institutions: universities, foundations, private associations, and government. Each has at least one distinctive function. The universities produce knowledge through teaching and scientific research. The foundations provide financial support to the universities and other population institutions. The private associations both provide services and attempt to influence elite and mass public opinion through public-relations and lobbying. And the government authorizes and finances many of the activities that the other institutions perform.

This combination of institutions, individuals, and resources is allied in pursuit of a common objective—the reduction of fertility to achieve a reduction in population growth, at home and abroad. The alliance is the Population Coalition. The coalition's goal has been articulated thus: ". . . Everything that properly can be done to lower population growth rates should be done, now."[25]

A combination of institutions and individuals employing a set of resources in pursuit of a common goal comprises a policy-making apparatus. In the population area, this apparatus is depicted by two figures: Figure 4-2 shows the locations of individuals and resources in the four types of institutions involved; Figure 4-3 shows the linkages among them.

In Chapter 1 we speculated about the increasing reliance upon technocrats in policy formulation. In the case of the population policy-making apparatus portrayed by Figures 4-2 and 4-3, we see an example of the commanding role that experts can play. Thus the Professional/Intellectuals, by their presence in all

| | | Institutional Bases | | | |
		University	Foundation	Private Association	Government
Individual Actors	Professional/ Intellectual	X	X	X	X
	Private Influential		X	X	
	Public Official				X
	Cerebral	X	X	X	X
	Influence		X	X	
Resources	Money		X		X
	Authority				X

Figure 4-2. The American Population Policy Formulation Process: Network of Actors and Resources

Figure 4-3. The American Population Policy Formulation Process: Network of Relationships

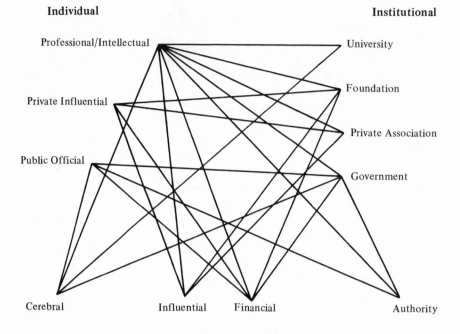

the institutions involved in the process, enjoy access to all the resources employed in policy formulation. Perhaps this is why the prominent scientists and intellectuals have been characterized by some of their peers as "mandarins" or "high priests."

Beyond the potential for simultaneous exercise of influence in several institutions and over several resources, as suggested by Figures 4-1 and 4-2, the scientists and intellectuals can act through a network of staff, and advisory or consulting assignments. These assignments involve participation on panels, boards, committees, and functioning as consultants for institutions outside the individual's principal place of employment. The purposes of the assignments, normally, are to advise on program and research strategy, evaluate research proposals, and to recommend research and fellowship grants, as well as other sorts of program funding. Thus, involvement in these activities permits an individual to influence the policy-making agenda at an early, and critical, stage.

To depict this network, we examined the spread of affiliations of Professional/Intellectuals who had more than a single staff/consulting/advisory affiliation with a prominent institution. For this purpose, we looked at staffs, the composition of boards, panels, committees, and consultantships in the following institutions in 1970:

> The Population Council
> The Ford Foundation
> Planned Parenthood/World Population
> Department of Health, Education and Welfare
> National Institutes of Health
> Agency for International Development
> Bureau of the Census
> National Academy of Sciences

This review disclosed that twenty-six scientists and professionals in the population field had affiliations with more than one institution. The range of affiliations of these individuals involved from two to five of the institutions. Sixteen of the twenty-six individuals had affiliations with the Population Council, either on the staff or as a member of one of its consulting or advisory committees. Interestingly, sixteen members of this group were employed by universities, four by foundations (the Population Council was classified as a foundation), three by the government, and one by a private association.[26]

Thus, a senior officer of the Population Council was simultaneously a consultant to the Ford Foundation and a member of AID's Population Advisory Group (the Population Council derives significant funding from both these institutions). A director of a major university population center served simultaneously on an advisory committee of the Population Council, on two review panels at the Center for Population Research (National Institutes of Health), on an advisory committee of the Bureau of the Census, and with the AID Population Advisory Group. A university professor served the Population Council in four capacities, was on an advisory council of Planned Parenthood/World Population, a consultant to the Ford Foundation, and with AID's Population Advisory Group. A board member of the Population Council served in the same capacities for the Ford Foundation, Planned Parenthood/World Population, and AID. An officer of Planned Parenthood/World Population served the Population Council in two capacities, in addition to being a member of AID's advisory group. A Ford Foundation staff member served with the AID advisory group, and on the Executive Committee of the National Academy of Science's Study of the Consequences of Population Change. A Rockefeller Foundation staff member served with the AID group and on the Bureau of the Census Advisory Committee on Population Statistics. And another university center director served in advisory capacities for the Population Council, the Center for Population Research, the Census Bureau, and AID.

Within the staff/advisory/consulting network the Professional/Intellectual community is linked in common enterprise with the principal sources of authority and resources—the government and the foundations. And, while the functions involved are formally advisory, the quality of a consultative role can be sufficiently influential to permit a definitive impact on authoritative decisions. At the least, channels of communications are available and abundant; at the most, they facilitate a consensual approach to decision-making among the counselors and those officially responsible for making the decisions.

While it is not possible to assess definitively the quality of the advisory roles, it is reasonable to assume that, in the aggregate, they are influential in determining the agendas, strategies, and related allocations of resources involved in American population policy formulation.

Donors and Recipients

The pivotal role of the Population Council in the intellectual sector is further illustrated by an analysis of the distribution of funds to American population institutions. The Population Council has evolved into a major funding conduit, as both a recipient and donor of funds. Though not a foundation itself, because it does not have a permanent endowment, the council functions as a foundation by distributing large grants for institution building, training, and research.

The analysis of funding covers the period 1956-1970, and reflects the distribution of funds from four major private-funding sources: the Rockefeller Brother's Fund, the Rockefeller Foundation, the Ford Foundation, and the Population Council; and the two major government sources, the Department of Health, Education and Welfare, and the Agency for International Development.

The analysis shows that forty-three American institutions received $225.4 million during the fourteen years reported. Of these institutions, ten received 66.5 percent of the funds. These top ten institutions are reflected in Figure 4-4. The Population Council received approximately 33 percent of the funds distributed to the major recipients. And, aside from Planned Parenthood/World Population, the remaining eight recipients are American universities.

The distribution of Population Council funds to American universities during this same time span (1956-1970) approximates the overall distribution reflected in Figure 4-4. Six of the top ten recipients from the leading private and public donors were among the top ten recipients of Population Council support:

> Rockefeller University
> University of Chicago
> Columbia University
> University of Michigan
> Johns Hopkins University
> University of California (Berkeley)[27]

Thus, as a conduit for institutional funding, the Population Council conforms to the overall funding pattern.

Figure 4-4. Leading Recipients of Funds 1956-1970

	Institution
1.	Population Council
2.	University of North Carolina
3.	Rockefeller University
4.	Columbia University
5.	University of Michigan
6.	Harvard University
7.	University of California (Berkeley)
8.	Johns Hopkins University
9.	Planned Parenthood/World Population
10.	University of Pennsylvania

Sources:
1) Annual Reports 1956-1970
   The Ford Foundation
   Rockefeller Brother's Fund
   The Rockefeller Foundation
   The Population Council
2) Agency for International Development–Office of Population, "Population Program Assistance," December 1971
3) Department of Health, Education and Welfare, Report of the Secretary, 5-Year Plan for Family Planning, October 1971

It is also of interest that members of nine of the ten leading institutional recipients of overall funding have multiple affiliations in the Staff/Advisory/Consulting network, which influences the allocation of financial resources for population activities.

Admittedly these are gross data, subject to a variety of interpretations. They are presented here to suggest, whatever the meaning, a convergence of the access routes to resources by individuals in positions to influence them in American population policy-making. This pattern, in itself, does not suggest a cabalistic relationship among the universities and the client/benefactors to whom they provide counsel, or that the advisors tend to distribute the action among themselves. It more likely suggests that, for various institutional reasons, a small group of specialists and their institutions have developed effective and recognizable capacities in population scholarship, research, and service. Thus, good money tends to follow good, and, as a result of their good work, the beneficiary institutions are the prime sources of good advisors who participate in the allocation of the good money. But, however, assessed, the resulting structures confer considerable influence upon the actors involved in determining the agenda of the American population policy-making, the phenomena to be examined, the data to be evaluated, the strategies to be followed, and the resources to be deployed.

The Population Council has been the leading American recipient of financing for population activities. Since its formation in 1952, the Council has received its major financial support from the Ford Foundation, the Rockefeller Foundation and family, and the Scaife family. Between 1952 and 1970, contributions from Rockefeller and Scaife sources totaled 48 percent of Population Council funding. The Ford Foundation contributed 34 percent, and U.S. Government sources 18 percent during this same period.[28] These funding sources supplied approximately 90 percent of the nearly $87 million made available to the Council during 1952-1970. The remaining 10 percent was contributed by a variety of private sources, including foundations and individuals.

Thus, nearly half of the Council's support during this eighteen-year time span came from two families prominent in the corporate sector of American society (the Scaifes are a branch of the Mellon family). In addition to the Rockefeller Foundation, Rockefeller contributions to the Population Council came from the Rockefeller Brother's Fund, Mrs. John D. Rockefeller Jr., Mrs. Jean Mauze (a sister of the Rockefeller brothers), John D. Rockefeller 3rd, and several other members of the family. The Scaife funding came from Mrs. Cordelia Scaife May and Mrs. Alan M. Scaife and family.

Funding Biases

Two categories of population activities have received support from American sources: (1) the creation and dissemination of knowledge (teaching and research); and (2) the utilization of knowledge to create change (action programs). These activities have been distributed among four identifiable fields: (1) *Family planning*—the provision of opportunities for making and implementing fertility choices; (2) *Non-family planning*—the provision of opportunities for making choices from all types of population conditions; (3) *Biomedical*—the utilization of biomedical knowledge and methods; (4) *Non-biomedical*—the utilization of knowledge and methods drawn from the humanities, social sciences, and other behavioral sciences. Choices about population activities—strategies, priorities, and the related allocation of resources are made within this pattern.

Supporters of population activities classify their programs in different ways, principally by distinguishing between the biomedical and non-biomedical. However, for a meaningful differentiation between the programs, it is necessary to distinguish between those directly in support of fertility regulation objectives, i.e., family planning, and those aimed at other goals.

A review of the strategies of the leading American donors suggests a marked preference for family-planning objectives sought mainly through the biomedical route.

Until the United States Government entered the field in the mid-sixties, the

Figure 4-5. Population Activities: Teaching/Research and Action Programs

	Biomedical	Non-biomedical
Family Planning		
Non-Family Planning		

Ford Foundation was the largest source of funding for population activities in the United States and abroad. From 1954, when the first Ford population grant was made to the Population Council, until 1971 Ford granted a total of $153.4 million in the population field. Of this total approximately 54 percent was spent for activities in reproductive biology and contraceptive development. The remaining 46 percent was allocated for non-biomedical programs in family planning and other population-related fields.[29]

The distribution of support by other major donors between the biomedical and non-biomedical activities reflects an emphasis more heavily weighted than Ford's in favor of priorities in reproductive biology and contraceptive development supporting of family-planning objectives. Thus, the Rockefeller Foundation allocated approximately 56 percent of its population resources to biomedicine, with another 38 percent to the closely related priority of family-planning-services program development. The Population Council spent approximately 40 percent of its resources for activities in biomedicine, another 36 percent for family-planning services, and 23 percent for social science research, a significant portion of it in support of family-planning strategies.

One of the explanations for the substantial Rockefeller Foundation and Population Council allocations in the biomedical field is their continuing commitment to Rockefeller University, which houses the Biomedical Division of the Population Council, one of the world's foremost research institutes in the field of reproductive physiology and contraceptive development.

U.S. government allocations in the population field also reflect a preference for family-planning program development and related activities in biomedicine. Institutional development and research support from government sources have been distributed approximately as follows: 68 percent for the biomedical and family-planning field, and 32 percent for other activities, many of which relate directly to family-planning priorities.[30]

The U.S. foreign aid program, administered by the Agency for International Development, has accorded priority to family planning. The distribution of AID support since 1965 is approximately 81 percent for family-planning activities, including research in reproductive physiology and contraceptive product development, and the creation of more effective contraceptive delivery systems; and 9 percent for activities not directly related to family-planning programs.[31] Within projects totaling $233 million between 1965-1971, $21.7 has been allocated for non-family-planning activities.

A Public Forum

The Commission on Population Growth and the American Future provided a unique forum in which prevailing population wisdom and action could be evaluated by representatives from a wide spectrum of American society. The Commission contained a broad representation from the public and private sectors of American society—Congress, business, labor, intellectual, female, and youth—and from institutions interested in population matters (see Figure 4-6). However, representation of the Population Coalition still was a dominant factor in the commission's makeup.

Of the original 24-member commission, eight individuals had interests in the population field in their professional or private capacities: three were associated with the private foundations that have been the major financial contributors in the field (Rockefeller/Rockefeller Foundation and Population Council, Bell/Ford Foundation, Berelson/Population Council); one was the board chairman of the major family-planning organization (Beasley/Planned Parenthood); one was a past president of the Population Association of America (Duncan); two were among the most energetic sponsors of population-related legislation in the Congress (Tydings and Packwood); and one was a member of a major population-interest group (Wood/Population Crisis Committee).

It was reasonable to assume that all conflicting positions and interests would be reflected in the commission membership. Among those groups directly interested in the proceedings were poor (black and white), black, and female sectors of the American public. In addition, the ecologists and critics of family planning had something to offer.

Four women were among the original commission appointees—two specialists in urban affairs and two housewives active in civic affairs. One of the women is active in the Chicano movement (Olivarez). A black woman (Mrs. Boswell) was

61

JOHN D. ROCKEFELLER 3RD
Chairman

GRACE OLIVAREZ
Executive Director, Food for all Inc.
Vice Chairwoman

CHRISTIAN N. RAMSEY, JR. M.D.
President, The Institute for the Study of Health and Society
Vice Chairman

JOSEPH D. BEASLEY, M.D.
President, Family Health, Inc.

ANTONIO LUIS FERRÉ[5]
President, Puerto Rican Cement Company, Inc.

DAVID E. BELL
Executive Vice President, The Ford Foundation

JOAN F. FLINT
Vice-Chairman
Tulsa City-County Library Commission

BERNARD BERELSON
President, The Population Council

R. V. HANSBERGER .
Chairman and President, Boise Cascade Corporation

JOHN A. BLATNIK[1]
United States Representative
8th District of Minnesota

D. GALE JOHNSON
Chairman, Department of Economics, University of Chicago

ARNITA LOUISE YOUNG BOSWELL[2]
Associate Professor, School of Social Service Administration
University of Chicago

JOHN R. MEYER
President, National Bureau of Economic Research

MARGARET BRIGHT
Professor, Dept. of Behavioral Sciences,
School of Hygiene and Public Health
The Johns Hopkins University

BOB PACKWOOD
United States Senator
Oregon

MARILYN BRANT CHANDLER
Board of Governors, Otis Art Institute

JAMES S. RUMMONDS
Student, Stanford School of Law

PAUL B. CORNELY, M.D.
Assistant to the Executive Medical Officer,
Welfare and Retirement Fund, United Mine Workers of America

STEPHEN L. SALYER
Student, Davidson College

ALAN CRANSTON[3]
United States Senator
California

HOWARD D. SAMUEL
Vice President, Amalgamated Clothing Workers of America

LAWRENCE A. DAVIS[4]
President, Arkansas Agricultural, Mechanical & Normal College

JAMES H. SCHEUER[6]
United States Representative
21st District of New York

OTIS DUDLEY DUNCAN
Professor of Sociology, University of Michigan

JOSEPH D. TYDINGS[7]
Former United States Senator
Maryland

JOHN N. ERLENBORN
United States Representative
14th District of Illinois

GEORGE D. WOODS
Director and Consultant, The First Boston Corporation

[1]Resigned Jan. 2, 1971
[2]Since Sept. 14, 1971
[3]Since Feb. 26, 1971

[4]Since Jan. 6, 1971
[5]Resigned April 6, 1971

[6]Since March 8, 1971
[7]Resigned Jan. 3, 1971

Figure 4-6. The Commission on Population Growth and the American Future

appointed as a substitute for an original member who resigned. But so far as can be determined, not one of the women was poor. And it is assumed that not one of the female commissioners was equipped by first-hand experience to represent the female constituency that uses publicly-supported family-planning services.

One black was among the original commission membership—Dr. Paul Cornely, Chairman of the Department of Community Health Practice at Howard University, and a past president of the American Public Health Association. In addition to Mrs. Boswell, another black member was added to replace an original appointee, Dr. Lawrence Davis, President of Arkansas Agricultural, Mechanical, and Normal College.

None of the male commissioners would be characterized as poor, and not one could be identified as representing a poverty-interest group.

While the family-planning position was well represented by commissioners from organizations which have supported it—the Population Council, Planned Parenthood/World Population, the Ford Foundation, and the Rockefeller Foundation—neither leading critics of the family-planning strategy, nor ecological critics were appointed to or represented on the commission; i.e., Paul Ehrlich, Garrett Hardin, Kingsley Davis, Judith Blake, or Barry Commoner. Nor was there any representation on the commission of the largest public-interest group concerned with population growth—Zero Population Growth.

Established positions were dominant, and challenging positions unrepresented in the first major public commission on American population policy. The fact that a family-planning philosophy and approach emerged as the dominant position in the commission's final report is, consequently, not difficult to understand.

5 Reflections of a Coalition

The Reflector

The preceding chapter described the American population coalition by identifying its components—principal actors, institutional and individual; linkages among them; and resources that fuel them. This chapter proceeds with a selective examination of how some participants in the coalition visualize their roles and mission.

To obtain this self-image, a series of interviews and discussions were conducted in 1970 with a cross section of thirty-six individuals identified as influential participants in the American population coalition.[1] These individuals were selected from the three major sectors of the coalition—intellectual, private, and public. They were identified on the basis of actual and potential influence within their particular sectors, and in the coalition as a whole.

Though it is constantly employed both in political analysis and investigative reporting with mixed results, the identification of influential individuals is a delicate process. No single method for doing so is likely to be adequate. Accordingly, investigative reporters and political analysts seek a mix of clues to the location of influence, including reputations among associates and other knowledgeables, positions occupied, and evidence of participation in the decision-making process.

By preliminary discussions, examinations of published material (scholarly and otherwise), and analysis of the scope of individual activities, a group of individuals was identified for the interviews and discussions reported herein. Some were classified as key persons in American population policy-making. The others were classified as representative influential individuals within their respective sectors. As a result of meetings with these preselected individuals, we enjoyed access to an adequate and representative cross section of influence within the population coalition. All sessions with the selected respondents were handled on an off-the-record basis, and, accordingly, their identity is disclosed neither here nor in the ensuing discussion.[3]

Interviewing influentials is complicated by several constraints, including the normal problem of access, limitations of time, duration of their attention span, and those restrictions they choose to impose on the subject under consideration, as well as upon the interview itself. In view of these realities, the interviewer must choose among alternatives; for example, reactions to a set of standard questions or reactions to questions about which the respondent is most knowledgeable. Whichever he selects, the interviewer should be guided by the approach likely to produce results of most value to his inquiry.

Since the enterprise reported here was exploratory, it seemed reasonable to involve the respondents in the exploration. They, after all, are involved in the universe under exploration, and thus well-suited to illuminate those parts most familiar to them. The total of these parts was likely to produce some semblance of a complete map. The alternative was to impose a set of standard questions constructed by an interviewer less familiar with the universe, and thus likely, in part, to be irrelevant to it.

Whatever the relative scientific merit of either approach, influentials, like most people, are bored with standard questionnaires. They like to talk about that which interests them most. And, however busy, they welcome the opportunity to expound upon their favorite subjects. As the interviewing proceeded, the technique selected was justified. Though not productive of what is normally classified as "hard data," it yielded a rich and relevant catch.[4]

The Vision

Sometimes explicit, but more frequently implicit, in the population dialogue that has evolved during the past decade is a concern for improved standards of individual and societal well-being. As the population movement developed a consensus concerning family planning as a first-stage remedy for dealing with excessive population growth, the welfare norm became increasingly taken for granted. With the problem diagnosed—excessive population growth, and the prognosis established—stabilizing and reducing it—the movement has become task-oriented and focused upon how best to do the job. The rationale for doing the job at all, or doing it in preference to other jobs, was accepted, or at least not questioned.

Yet, considering the variety of individuals and groups active in the American population coalition, it is likely to assume a variety of motivations, preferences, and visions of individual and societal welfare. The civic-minded members of private associations, for example, are busy individuals confronted by many demands for their good works, and numerous opportunities for tangible expression of their civic-mindedness. The professional/intellectuals, with the exception of the demographers to whom population change is a stock-in-trade, are confronted by an array of channels through which their professional skills and interests may be expressed. And members of Congress experience spirited bidding from many quarters for some portion of their legislative attention. What brings all of them together in this particular common cause?

The configuration of individuals and groups that has coalesced would appear somewhat anomalous. What, if any, is the common utopian model that united the student liberals in Zero Population Growth with the captains of industry in the Population Crisis Committee? What is the quality of common cause that created a Congressional alliance for energetic family planning legislation, ranging an ideological spectrum from James Scheuer, on the liberal pole, to George Bush, on the conservative?[5] What are the common social visions that join Professor Philip Hauser and Dr. Reinhold Niebuhr with Lammot duPont Copeland (E.I. duPont de Nemours & Co., Inc.) and George Champion (The Chase Manhattan Bank) in the group.

To explore the ultimate objectives of representatives of this varied group, their reactions to three issues were sought: (1) the goals of individual and social well-being, in whose name population change should be manipulated; (2) the significance of population change as a propellant or obstacle to the goals; and (3) the type of manipulation that should be considered.

Reactions to this group of issues revealed both something of the individual world view and the reason for personal involvement in population matters. Concerning ultimate purpose, more than half of the responses were clustered about the classic liberal notion of providing people with the opportunity to achieve an improved quality of life, with the related advantages for both the individual and the community. Several respondents, involved in developing population activities outside the United States, viewed political stability as a desirable rationale for efforts to control population growth. Internal stabilization was seen as a critical requirement for the positive and harmonious growth of less-developed societies. Four respondents felt a need for changes in the structure of societies—how societies are organized to distribute opportunities and advantages, and who has a say in the process—as a requirement for higher levels of individual and communal well-being. They visualized the control of population growth, in the United States and abroad, as a means to accelerate the changes that would bring a better distribution of opportunity for greater numbers of people.

Thus, the respondents who reflected and were articulate about their view of ultimate purpose visualized an improved condition of life as within the capacity of mankind. They expressed their preferences in non-ideological terms—in a pragmatic, goal-oriented, humanitarian framework whose ingredients comprised such qualities as "freedom," "higher quality of life," "opportunities," "gradual change," and "stability." All saw population growth as an obstacle to the achievement of their favorite vision, some as a major obstacle demanding priority treatment, and others as one of a number of significant obstacles, all of which required energetic handling.

As for the prescription and delivery of remedies, only four respondents suggested a need now for measures that would coerce changes in individual fertility behavior. Three of these were public officials, and one a private influential. All others who reacted to this issue expressed a preference for the traditional family-planning approach—illumination of the issue, dissemination of knowledge and technology, and exercise of individual choice.

A selection of individual responses yielded an interesting array of concerns, and some detail on how the participants view their purpose.

One of the most prominent professional/intellectuals in the population movement emphasized that population control is not a final value:

... population policy is a question of means, not ends, in which the value of children is one of the values ...

He maintained that calculation of related costs and benefits involved in this value should be influenced by an ethic composed of several components, including a trans-generational quality:

1. Effective personal freedom in fertility behavior;
2. The provision of full information on fertility behavior, taking into account social and individual consequences;
3. Both of the foregoing, to the end of maintaining generational options. . . . We must not close off options for succeeding generations ...

A black executive of a Planned Parenthood affiliate in a major city expressed a broad purpose:

... a domestic population program must be part of a bigger effort to elevate the quality of life ...
... if the quality-of-life problem is ignored in favor of family planning, the only difference is that there will be fewer people in those substandard houses ...
... blacks and Puerto Ricans are naturally desirous of small families; but they fall out of the opportunity structure that encourages small-family perform-ance . . as a result, a psychology of indifference develops ...

A private influential with a long-standing involvement in the population movement sensed churnings in the developing countries:

... there is a growing pressure from below for improvements ...
... population growth is an obstacle to other measures that might create an improved society ...
... the leadership has a crucial role to play in recognizing this link ...

As for the United States, he maintained that young people have played an important role:

... through their interest in the environment and ecology, the young have put the problem on the map ...

Two public officials sensed perils of instability resulting from excessive population growth in developing countries:

... the implications of population growth on political stability, and the implications of friction between countries ...

... there are no insuperable problems about feeding more people as technology develops. The major problem is living together ... how people can live together peacefully and productively ... the more they impinge on one another ... there is a shortening of space and time differentials ... highly explosive ...

In the search for possible remedies to these conditions, one exposed a common conviction:

... the conclusion should be that growth should be controlled ...

A private influential saw the familiar domestic trauma as a basis for population concerns:

... education; pollution; urban concentration; pressure on the cities; blacks flock to the cities ...
... population growth compounds all these problems ...

Another influential private leader expressed confidence that the problem of domestic growth would be solved, and saw the major growth problem overseas. Nevertheless, he stated:

... we must go beyond voluntarism in dealing with U.S. growth ...

Others viewed the population issue and its related goals in terms other than growth. Two university-based professional/intellectuals, presently functioning as public officials, articulated different dimensions of domestic population phenomena:

... the population problem is more one of distribution than growth ...
... zero population growth is a lot of crap ... not the correct objective ... if we had the density of Holland we could get all our people into Rhode Island ...
... we need to build a calculation of population change into American government ... into the allocation of government resources and the making of decisions ... this consciousness leads to (informed) consideration of problems such as educational finance; questions of optimum population, such as when does democracy get too big to handle? ... the lower classes having more children than they want ...

Another two university-based members of the professional/intellectual sector shared visions of a more just and creative society, and perceived obstacles to it other than those created by population growth:

... equalization of opportunity in the U.S.; for example, in education and employment, not just to earn, but to improve the quality of life ... and an equalization of opportunity between the U.S. and the developing world ...
... a more just society ... a higher regard for human rather than material

values . . . creation of a heterogeneous society with a premium on cultural pluralism . . . perhaps along the lines of socialism—Swedish style . . .

. . . population distribution is the major problem . . . seek a distribution policy that would provide adequate low- and middle-income housing, a desegregation of suburbia, the building of small planned cities . . . and a transportation policy consistent with the distribution policy . . .

As for the obstacles to their visions, they saw:

. . . the power distribution . . . a concentration of power in a power elite . . . an alliance between middle America and the industrial complex, supporting a middle-American syndrome which is racist . . . parochial, and materialistic.

. . . nature of the free enterprise system . . . vested interests of a free enterprise economy . . . affluence . . . absence of national control . . .

. . . insular psychology of Americans with respect to their international responsibilities . . . closing the gap between developed and developing countries . . .

Legislators reflected less global concerns. One discovered "population" as a result of the 1968 campaign:

. . . found interest in the environment . . . because of the structure of the (*legislative body in which he sits*) had to relate environment to something other than pollution . . . so did the connection to population . . . "

Another, who eschewed political benefits from his involvement, moved through similar channels:

. . . started with pollution . . . led to population . . . sees population growth pressuring the environment . . . face political danger of becoming a one-issue man . . . "

A third, similarly, reported no political cost/benefit analysis:

. . . a matter of conviction . . . social friends were interested in Planned Parenthood . . . after election, called Planned Parenthood . . . trip to Latin America dramatized issue . . . became fanatic on issue . . .

Some professional/intellectuals in the federal government saw their mission based on an opportunity norm; in one case opportunity both for the federal government, and for the public beneficiaries:

. . . concern for family planning emerged . . . because of recognition of unequal access to health services by poor . . . family planning was recognized as a cheap potentially effective program for the poor . . . it did not require an enormous investment of health manpower . . .

Another reflected on the scope of opportunity, and, eventually, the terms upon which it might have to be provided:

... there should be no unserved and unknowledgeable people in the U.S. ... opportunity should exist to determine size of family on a voluntary basis ... sterilization and abortion should be offered on a voluntary basis ... someday we have to go to control—the issue is who controls whom ...

A third saw the boundaries of government intervention as fixed:

... the guiding norm is voluntary ... we have a policy based on voluntarism ...

Some respondents volunteered reactions and interpretations of the positions of other actors, individual and institutional:

On the sudden attractiveness of the population issue to financial supporters, a government-based professional/intellectual suggested the grounds for their interest:

... it is highly visible ... it can clearly be pointed out as a need ... they see crowding, slums, pollution, and the like, and they relate these things to population growth ...

The focus on developing countries, particularly during the early days of U.S. concern for population growth, was explained by a professional/intellectual associated with a private association:

... dealing with the domestic problem would create controversy; for instance the church was willing to overlook programs far away ... and inadequacies in other systems would be uncovered—for instance in domestic health-delivery systems and in the universities ... therefore programs using overseas countries as laboratories ...

Concerning the origin of support to the population movement in the United States, another professional/intellectual associated with a private association maintained that:

... the population issue was a taxpayer's revolt against welfare ... this results in support from conservatives and southerners ...

At the same time, this respondent argued that to be credible:

... the origin of political support should be liberal ...

The linkage of population to problems of the environment was assessed by two foundation-based professional/intellectuals:[6]

... the tie-in with the environment is dangerous for the population field . . . it is exaggerated . . .
... the environmentalists are willing to accept impairment of traditional human rights . . . they neglect all other elements in the environment other than ecology . . . poverty not prosperity depletes resources . . . pollution is a problem of gross economic mismanagement . . .

Those who advocate population control were evaluated by a Planned Parenthood executive:

... there is a lack of human compassion on the part of the population zealots . . .

And a white Planned Parenthood leader recognized the skepticism of "sophisticated black leaders," who raise the question:

... why are they getting so interested in our fertility when they are not interested in anything else? . . .

On the attempt of a major foundation to settle on a common rationale for its involvement in population matters, a foundation-based professional/intellectual disclosed:

... there is an internal debate on the principal objective: birth control or human welfare . . .

Though a highly-intellectualized foundation may feel compelled to sort out the normative ingredients for its involvement in population-related activities, the preoccupation is by no means universal among individual and institutional actors.[7] The normative image that emerges from discussions with those involved is opaque—human welfare is birth control, and birth control is human welfare. There may be variations within the priorities, for example, in which ingredients of human welfare come first. But, for the most part, the pattern for all consists of the same basic ingredients, all related to opportunities for social and economic elevation. There was but one exception to this standard mix, which was posed by the two professional/intellectuals who suggested that system transformation might belong in the package, i.e., changes in the distribution of power within the prevailing political and economic systems.

It should not be surprising that system transformation does not enter the calculus of ultimate goals for most participants in the population coalition. By virtue of their positions and roles in society, they are central participants in the system. And while they might not favor its configuration at a given time, they do not regard a disagreeable configuration as fixed, because, among other things, they feel confident and capable of arranging desirable modifications.

Their favorite images merge in a standard mix of educated middle-class concerns. And whatever the marginal variations in their images and concerns, they tend to be largely accepting of one another's, as they work together in the population cause. Something good can be accomplished by the manipulation of human fertility; no need to dwell at length on what and why. The benefits for all concerned have been sorted out. How an individual or institution arrives at his calculus of the benefits is of little concern. There are enough benefits to suit everyone's favored vision. And, the population issue serves as a neutralizing agent for conflicts that might otherwise arise from variations in the visions.

Accordingly, a consensual attitude has emerged that tends to prevent consideration of alternatives other than manipulation of human fertility as better routes to greater opportunities for a better life.

The Route

In reacting to the proceedings of the first international conference on family planning programs in 1965, Philip Hauser laid down a challenge to look beyond the agenda of remedies and prophesies that partisans of family planning were developing:

... the possible quarrel with the present family-planning movement is not with what it is attempting to do or with what it is doing. It is rather with what it is failing to do. It is failing to explore or to administer longer-range as well as the short-range programs against the possibility that its fundamental assumptions and basic premise ... may prove to be erroneous. The family-planning movement is failing to insure itself against the failure of its present rationale and methods. This is dangerous because at the present time it is not known whether the direct approach being used will in fact turn out to be a short cut in inducing social change. It is not yet known whether a birth control clinic will, in fact, bring about a more rapid decline in birth rate than improved and universal general education, or new roads facilitating communication, or improved agricultural methods, or a new industry that would increase productivity, or other types of innovations that may break the 'cake of custom' and produce social foment.[8]

Thus, Hauser's challenge pertained both to the efficacy of remedies to curb population growth, and to the efficiency of restraining population growth as a tool for achieving higher levels of individual and communal well-being.

A discourse concerning the alternatives to influence upon, or manipulation of, fertility behavior to achieve population limitation objectives is in an early stage.

However, alternatives to family planning are suggested from several vantage points. Considering the condition of the black community in the United States, Carl Flemister argues that reduction of population growth rates will not in itself raise the quality of life, and cites the paradox of government willingness to mount massive birth-control projects in the face of its failure to confront the problems of hunger, disease, and other social pathologies. In calling for research on social policy and social indicators, Charles Arnold and Philip Hauser suggest the potential for exploring approaches to other than direct fertility manipulation to respond to the needs of U.S. blacks.[10] The potential of manipulating conditions in the social and economic environment is suggested by Commoner:

... between the biological initiation and the biological end result, the process (fertility regulation) is mediated by a social factor, the awareness by the society of a satisfactory future, which motivates control of fertility ... the crucial factor which leads to a reduction in fertility—economic and social well-being.[11]

As a result of his work in Colombia and Puerto Rico, Schultz provides empirical validation for Commoner's position. In Colombia, he concluded that wider dissemination of basic education, improved employment opportunities for females, and better maternal-child health services promise to reduce fertility indirectly.[12] And, similarly, in Puerto Rico, he found an indirect association between fertility and relative earnings capacity of men and women in the labor force.[13] Kuznets adds the dimension of political and social power, arguing that the system for distributing rewards in society is equal in importance to that of economic resources in influencing fertility.[14]

Though the analyses of Commoner, Schultz, Nerove, and Kuznets dealt with less-developed societies, they could be applicable equally to less-developed enclaves within developed societies: for example, the enclave that concerned Flemister, Arnold, and Hauser.

Thus, granted the ultimate objective of elevating human welfare, should the manipulation of fertility be ranked systematically in the order of available techniques? And if so, what role should the Population Coalition play in the evaluatory process?

There was little inclination by most respondents to come to grips with the issue of alternatives. On the part of some, there were symptoms of impatience about the matter being raised at all. Evidently Hauser's challenge had made little impact since its issuance three years before. There was little evidence of systematic thinking about alternatives. The coalition's task orientation seemed to have steered it into a categorical approach, as if to say: "Fertility control is my bag; let somebody else worry about the other." And when approaches other than fertility manipulation were suggested, they most frequently were proposed as complementary components of the "better-life" package than as substitutes for fertility manipulation in achieving control of population growth.

Though more than half of those who reacted to the relevance of alternative approaches agreed that options other than the manipulation of fertility existed, few displayed a concern for the adequacy with which alternate remedies were being sought systematically by individuals and institutions equipped for the enterprise. There was an inclination to categorize separately the options for reducing population growth from those required for improvements in communal well-being. In any case, there was little evidence of concern that the population movement should be involved with the quest for substitutes for its familiar kit. There was more concern about the mechanics for likely alternatives—the absence of research tools, the distinctive missions and roles of organizations, and even, if feasible, the magnitude of resources required for substitutes to fertility manipulation.

There was a noticeable preference for slicing the job, as it is presently conceived, into manageable pieces with which the Population Coalition would deal with the sector for which it is most qualified—the reduction of human fertility. Where alternatives were idenitifed, whether as complements or substitutes for direct fertility manipulation, they spanned a familiar range of generality and specificity: a general expansion of the opportunity structure for deprived individuals and classes; the provision of specific opportunities for more adequate education, employment, and housing; a more sensitive and rational treatment of the physical environment in the interest of individual and communal betterment; the removal of obstacles to social mobility; and the necessary restructuring of political systems to facilitate all these improvements.

In response to the question of whether a narrow interpretation of its universe suggests that the Population Coalition is afflicted with a *status-quo* bias in accepting prevailing conditions of society as fixed, a foundation-based professional/intellectual replied:

... we're invited not to create social revolution, but to provide expertise ... social revolution has not affected fertility behavior in Algeria and Tanzania ... (my organization) has to remain immune (to charges of tampering with social structures) ...

Another foundation-based professional/intellectual appraised the relationship of family planning and social change:

... family planning is a discrete area ... a family-planning program in itself can create structural changes in a society ... for example, in a Moslem society it can be upsetting to the *status quo* ... the introduction of a family-planning program is in itself an engine of social change ...

The same respondent suggested constraints the movement should set for itself:

... (we) are interested in principle in a broader focus ... but it would be a mistake to move too far afield ... principally because of funds limitations . . . there is a need to bring family planning up to the level of other economic development instruments . . . for developing countries family planning is not in serious competition with other development activities . . .

A professional/intellectual based in the government viewed alternatives as limited to those available for perfecting a fertility manipulation package, such as improving means of contraception and the delivery of services. As for the broader issues:

. . . the alternatives are processed at a very high level . . . there is no systematic examination . . . the process is compartmentalized . . . (our) choices are made between service and research . . .

Along the same lines, a university-based professional/intellectual currently in the government observed:

. . . without abortion and sterilization, family planning is unlikely to accomplish zero growth . . . sterilization and abortion should be supplied on a voluntary basis . . . the question is how to do it in a political setting . . . there are not many options available .,. . just a few years to make voluntarism work . . .

Another public official saw the alternatives as those involved in

. . . how to employ U.S. government resources to catalyze and push (fertility control) programs . . .

A public official in the legislative branch felt that options are limited by the real world of choice, which did not permit their rational calculation:

. . . there is no planning in the American system . . .
. . . if population is thought important, do something about population . . .

Another official in Congress contended:

. . . the population issue has not yet achieved the visibility to create a consciousness to evaluate options; for example, education versus family planning . . .

There were critical reactions to the categorical approach. A professional/ intellectual in a private association attributed this condition to inadequacies in the national dialogue on population matters:

. . . the U.S. has not had a debate on population policy . . . the noise has come from extremist groups with deficient knowledge . . . there is confusion in the field . . . policy-makers cannot divorce the dealing with unwanted pregnancies from other aspects . . .

A university-based professional/intellectual, temporarily in government service, saw the limited dialogue on population matters as a function of government failure:

... government doesn't pay attention to the fact (population change) ... toy manufacturers know more about the demographic profile ...

Another professional/intellectual in the government faulted restrictions imposed on the research agenda dealing with population change:

... exclusion of a broader focus by the intellectual value-system of those who dominate the setting of research priorities ... plus emphasis on elegance of design and credentials of researchers rather than on the value of subject matters ...

Though consideration of the alternatives to fertility manipulation was recognized as a potentially useful enterprise, there was evidence of a reluctance to do so because of practical problems.
An influential individual attributed the limitations to the absence of objectives:

... we really don't know what desired national goals are ...

A foundation-based professional/intellectual cited the difficult intellectual problems with the area he considered inadequately explored:

... hard to do ... we have attempted to get economic demographers to focus on this sort of question ... the objective is to find out more about social factors influencing population change ... one of the problems is the order of magnitude required for different objectives; for example, the needs for mass education in order to accomplish anything ...

Another professional/intellectual reacted to the possible calculus of costs and benefits among possible alternatives:

... a fallacious conception that there is a trade off between family-planning money and other social programs ... the price-tag's differential on fundamental welfare measures is enormous ... we have no research base to process the trade offs ...

And, speculating on the means of costing-out trade offs in developing countries, a foundation staff member posed the problem:

... would money devoted to steel plants do the job? ...

Another professional/intellectual from a foundation admitted the difficulty of coming to grips with alternatives:

. . . it makes sense . . . but the professionals don't do it because they don't know how . . .

There was recognition of the reality that the prevailing political system limited the range of options that realistically might be considered.

A university-based professional/intellectual accepted the need to study fertility manipulation:

. . . because of the nature of the economic and political system . . . the influence of monopolistic type industry . . . makes other options very difficult . . .

Another professional/intellectual associated with a university suggested requirements for broader alternative approaches:

. . . a change in the organization of power in American government . . . force responsibility on the part of American industry . . .

And an executive from a private association identified a significant obstacle within the system:

. . . the people calling the shots are removed from the people affected . . . lobbyists and vested interests are the only ones around calling the shots . . .

As examples of alternatives deserving of exploration, a foundation executive suggested:

. . . the reduction of (fertility) rates is no panacea . . . (we) are working on other options, in the areas of agriculture and education . . .

A professional/intellectual from a private association identified characteristics of the "sweat factor" for the poor as the total pattern of obstacles in their lives:

. . . consider the capacity of the poor in even getting to a (family planning) clinic . . . transportation, somebody to leave the kids with . . .

The restraints of the population-research structure as a key factor in creating broader dimensions for the policy discourse was cited by several professional/intellectuals interested in the potential of a broader discourse:

. . . (our) panels don't like programmatic research . . . they take the traditional approach to research which values hypothesis testing. . .
. . . there is a need for multi-centric research funding to avoid screening out some of the options . . . (we) have a different sort of research approach . . . a manipulative approach to research—how to achieve change . . .

... (our) reluctance about social science research till now was due to its "action orientation" ...

... (they) take a restricted view of social science research which is not goal-oriented ...

Though their existence is conceded, in a more or less abstract form, the alternatives to fertility control still appear to be peripheral in the orientation of some influential participants in the American Population Coalition. Options tend to be weighed more as differential ingredients of the fertility control approach than as a series of different approaches, all containing ingredients of potentially equal, or better, effectiveness.

If a collective feeling can be ascribed to a movement, the American Population Coalition feels a sense of urgency about its mission. It frankly admits that its capacities are less than fully developed, and its resources and knowledge less than abundant. It evinces a determination to improve and perfect the job it knows best, believing that this job is worthwhile.

This condition best explains its reluctance to venture too far afield. And while its reluctance might appear to be a form of professional self-satis-faction—satisfaction that the course is set, the targets established, and the assignments distributed—it is not. There is little evidence of complacency, particularly among the professional/intellectuals who dominate the population coalition. On the contrary, the evidence in individual discussions and in the written record suggests a continuing enterprise in professional soul-searching, a genuine sensitivity to the delicacy and complexity of the mission in which the Coalition is involved, and to the means for achieving its objectives.

But, while there is recognition that alternatives to the manipulation of fertility might exist, there is a basic reluctance to employ the Population Coalition as an arena in which to grapple with the options. There is recognition of a natural division of labor among the institutions concerned with treating the ills of society. And this position is justified, it is claimed, largely by the prevailing constraints upon resources—knowledge, skills, finances, and time—that suggest the wisdom of specialization. Population specialists, in other words, make their optimal contribution in dealing with population problems as they conceive them. And, while still in the abstract, there is almost universal recognition among leading participants in the Coalition that an effective prognosis for the ills of society involves some changes in the fabric of society, they visualize fertility control as a powerful agent in creating the conditions from within which the required structural changes can evolve.

The Corporate Structure

The American Population Coalition was described by some of its leading participants as "a symbiotic system," "incestuous," "a Mafia-like structure," "a tight little community," "a rich man's club," and "an interlocking directorate."

These characterizations suggest qualities that would buttress the consensual condition of the coalition suggested in the preceding sections. They also conjure up an institutional image that is exclusive, restrictive, noncompetitive, elitist, self-sustaining, and, perhaps, even conspiratorial. Though, admittedly, the coalition deals with matters of concern in the lives of the mass of citizens, this visualization does not suggest a forum which is particularly inviting to the expression of mass concerns.

But how important is a more popular forum, in this area or any other, especially when those who function in the more restricted forum do so skillfully, sensitively and in a manner largely supportive of the concerns and requirements of those who do not have direct access to the forum? And if the forum were enlarged, would the alteration necessarily increase its capacity to function effectively? Would more people engaged in a more complex communications network enhance the quality of the forum and its output? And, would the approach change? Would there be, say, a shift in objectives and priorities?

Finally, does an assessment of structure have any payoff? Is there merit in the Coalition's taking stock of how it is assembled?

These issues were examined by means of responses to questions that were focused upon: (1) the representative character of the American Population Coalition—its composition and accessibility; (2) the adequacy of the structure—the configuration of individuals, groups, and relationships—for handling the issues and problems it had delimited in its sphere of activity; and (3) the quality of membership of the Commission on Population Growth and the American Future.[15]

Though respondents depicted a restricted corporate-like structure, there was little evidence of concern among them that this condition significantly affected their capacity for policy-making. All who responded saw themselves involved in an identifiable aggregation, entry to which was limited by professional skill and reputation—other forms of achievement including civic preeminence, and simple evidence of concern for a common cause. But none of the factors which limited participation in the apparatus were perceived by most participants as significant constraints upon their perspective, sensitivity to the relevant issues, and intellectual and operational capabilities for achieving its objectives. The built-in exclusivities yielded both costs and benefits. On the positive side, there was the ease of communication, the continuing knowledge of who was doing what, the opportunities for cooperation and harmonious endeavor, and, as a result of all these qualities, a more rational allocation of total resources available to the coalition.

Negative features, for the most part, included those commonly associated with institutions to which entry is limited: inbreeding, parochialism, and organizational rivalries. But, to the extent that these qualities existed, they were symptoms more than real obstacles to performance. The participants involved were aware of them, and the coalition was capable of self-corrective action in dealing with them.

There was a consensus among respondents about the closeness and closedness of the population-policy apparatus. Each viewed these qualities from the experience encountered within his particular role. Thus, among some professional/intellectuals, there was a noticeable concern for the impact of this condition on research and operational strategies.

A foundation staff member described the environment:

. . . there is close easy cooperation at the staff level . . . we don't constrain each other on projects . . . we communicate them around . . . there are shared attitudes, for example to make voluntary family planning work better, but a concern with what to do beyond it . . . this commonality of attitudes might be characterized as "middle-of-the-road" . . . there is communication among the individuals involved . . . but the question arises: Is there too much commonality of identity? . . . Berelson is a key influencer of strategy . . .

A foundation officer observed:

. . . (I) know every demographer in the U.S. . . . there is some interaction among us . . . (I) more often ask the question: Shouldn't there be more cooperation? . . . it is a healthy thing to have independent inputs . . . the overlap of our boards is small . . . (I) don't see a deliberate split-up of the globe among the institutions . . .

A foundation staff member reflected on the determination of research strategies:

. . . research is a tight little professional community . . . the determination of priorities is made by members of the professional community in intimate dialogue with one another . . . Ford and Rockefeller pick up special things that NIH cannot do; for example, the more flexible things . . . product research falls in AID . . . it is directed at contraceptive development and is applied, rather than the basic research that NIH does . . .

A public official reflected on how the "tight little community" develops:

. . . there is a movement in and out of one role or another, academia to government, to foundations, etc. . . . channels of communication develop . . . and can lead to specialization in particular issues . . . one man can have great influence . . . a "mafia-like" structure has existed . . .

The influence of one man was noted by several professional/intellectuals:

. . . Draper is a key man . . . [16] there is nobody State would listen to more than Draper . . . he has gotten the message out, but is ineffective in developing remedies . . . the Drapers can generate the money, but not the remedies . . . because they can get commitments of money, they think they know how to spend it . . .
      . . . Draper's great contribution was to show that thinking big can be

done . . . but he is not program-oriented . . . he can communicate need for money, but can't say what should be done with it . . .

. . . Draper's organization and secretariat has been the most effective thing I have seen . . . they have changed the tide of decisions with timely intervention, such as phone calls and contracts with Congressmen . . . [17]

Another professional/intellectual based in the government found the "tight little community" resistant to both changes in strategy and entry of new strategists:

. . . there was blockage and resentment of OEO innovation by IPPF (International Planned Parenthood Federation), and the Population Council was resentful of AID efforts abroad . . . the Population Council and IPPF are showing signs of stodginess . . . a bureaucratic syndrome which results in misguided energies . . . traditional organizations like the Population Council are unable to translate policies into action . . . in HEW the vested interests, like NICHD, tried to capture the money . . . this set back family planning . . . it was subjected to the internal byzantine politics of HEW . . . [18]

There were misgivings expressed about the neglect of potentially promising research strategies, due to structural rigidities and related corporate sensitivities:

. . . there is a restriction upon the (behavioral) research agenda because of its control by demographers . . .

. . . the (HEW) research agenda is determined by the professional bias of CPR (Center for Population Research) . . .

. . . the single most significant failure is the neglect of research . . . (because) people don't want to push others around, such as set agendas for the medical community . . .

. . . the need for a more coherent research strategy is resisted by the academic community because they don't like to be structured . . .

Public officials with responsibility for population matters, but not themselves professional specialists, expressed another set of perceptions on the tightness of the structure:

. . . never fool with professional demographers . . . they limit the creative thinking process by their biases . . . demographers have snowed a lot of people . . . they have a jargon of their own . . . the commonsense approach is the best . . .

. . . there is a collegial reality to policy development . . . knowledge is in short supply . . . there is the need to learn and act simultaneously . . .

. . . support of the population movement traditionally comes from wealthy people . . .

Private influentials agreed with the characterization of structural intimacy, but did not regard it as a significant quality. One described it as a passing phase in a transition from private concern to public policy-formulation:

... relatively few have been concerned with population stabilization ... it is a small group but growing ... the concern so far has been reflected in the efforts of individuals, principally ... but there has been no policy-formulation process ... Congress and the young represent new interested groups ...

An officer of a private association described the profile of his organization:

... it is not a mass organization ... it is made up of successful people ... the linkages are personal as well as official ... there is no attempt to exclude other opinions ... the Hill is the place to register other opinions ...

The same private influential suggested how the opinions of the professional/ intellectuals were registered:

... they are folded into the boards of IPPF and the other organizations ...

The reactions depicted thus far are largely of an intramural character, concerns about relationships among individuals and groups already on the "inside" of the apparatus. There was some evidence of concern about the desirability of looking outward to sensitize the structure to a greater variety of viewpoints. Some of these concerns were expressed abstractly.

A foundation executive, for example, admitted:

... it would be a healthy thing to have some independent inputs ...

And another foundation executive looked over the horizon:

... we are in the foothills of a great debate about population policy ... it will eventuate in a determination of the issues that should be considered ... there are efforts to reach for a rational set of policies ... (the existing structure is able to handle the debate) but unevenly and imperfectly ...

Others were voiced in more concrete terms. A university-based professional/ intellectual suggested that the parochial quality of the apparatus limited exchanges with widely-differentiated, but potentially-interested groups in communities, on the state and local levels, and in the business community:

... the (professional/intellectual) arguments do not reach these groups ... they (the professional/intellectuals) are talking to each other ...

A private association executive suggested that:

... the Population Council-types are global in their thinking ... if they could only get close enough to the issues ... we need an outreach strategy—a rational involvement of people ...

A government executive valued OEO programs because they achieve an involvement of people:

> ... through community advisory boards at the local level, the consumer of services has a voice in the provision of the services . . .

To the extent that they reflect on the matter, or respond to questions about it, the actors are conscious of working within a corporate structure. But there appears to be little evidence of inclination on their part to evaluate the structure on other than operational terms, such as: How well does it work in performing the job at hand? And, to the extent that it does not work as effectively as they think it should, they appear to be confident that the corporation itself is capable of self-corrective action.

Thus, concerns about corporate structure emerge in terms of desirable internal adjustments, such as the tuning and rearranging of parts, rather than as requirements for changes in structural composition, charter, and membership. They are standard concerns common to large organizations: differential distributions of influence among traditionalists and innovators, necessary improvements in internal channels of communication, roles and status of individuals, and more effective ordering and performance of product research. These are adjustments, it is felt, most effectively handled by those already inside the organization.

The actors appear to feel comfortable within the structure as they now know it. They are aware of one another's position, role, and status. All are easily accessible to each other. Everyone knows what everyone else is doing and thinking, and why, because each has informed the other on numerous occasions through familiar channels of communication. There are few secrets, because secrets are difficult to maintain within intimate structures. The agenda is open for all who have access to it.

There is evidence of some concern, though not much, for involvement of those outside the structure who are affected by what it does. These are the consumers of the product the corporation assembles—the structure's public constituency. But the major concern is to obtain an accurate picture of consumer preference for the product, and the translation of this preference into an improved product able to attract more consumers. And, as in most market research, the preference is ascertained by methods developed by experts in the corporate structure. Direct participation of consumers in research design is not seen by most in the structure as particularly helpful. Besides, there is evidence of corporate confidence in existing methods for effective determination of consumer preference. Perhaps not all agree with a fellow corporation member that "their wants are known," but there seems to be general agreement that corporate members are sufficiently sensitive to "their wants" so that "they" will be adequately represented without "their" direct involvement in the corporate activities affecting them.

A word of explanation is in order for raising the issue of membership in the Commission of Population Growth and the American Future. The commission was the first citizen's body created specifically to grapple with the impact of population growth in American society. The charter of the commission envisioned the consequences of population growth as society-wide in scope. Accordingly, it would have been reasonable to assess the potential value of taking direct soundings, and obtaining direct reactions from all sectors of American society, to whatever agenda the commission chose to pursue. This capability, if significant, would have required a broadly-representative membership within the Commission. (The commission membership with its dominant representation from the Population Coalition was discussed in Chapter 4.)

Also, presumably the commission would have been likely to consider the ingredients of national population policy as it exists currently. Then (1970) as now, the only identifiable and explicit American policy for direct manipulation of population growth is the position on family planning announced by the President in 1969 and reflected in the Family Planning Act.[19] The national family planning-policy envisions the provision of the opportunity for determination of family size to all Americans. The principal beneficiary of this policy is an estimated population of five million American females, deprived of the opportunity unless it is provided for through publicly-subsidized facilities. Accordingly, it is legitimate to inquire into the desirability of representation from this client-group on a representative citizen's panel evaluating American population policy. To the extent that national family-planning policy is considered, their firsthand experiences could have illuminated the proceedings. And their preferences for public subsidization within their particular orders of priority—whether opportunities to plan families, or opportunities to plan something else—might have contributed a useful dimension to the deliberations.

There was little inclination by the policy-makers to react to the representative quality of the policy-making apparatus, as symbolized by the makeup of the commission. To the extent that interested individuals were not directly involved within the structure, their requirements and preferences were available as a result of empirical evaluations, or through less systematic but, nevertheless, valid soundings, such as community meetings.

Concerning the symbolic issue of commission membership, few of those who reacted saw the absence of a black, or poor, female as a deficiency. And, among those who did, the reaction tended to be one of surprise by an oversight by those who selected the commission members, rather than any reservation about the substantive merits of the issue.

A leading professional/intellectual in the government defined the issue of black/poor representation:

... you mean the absence of a black counterpart to Mrs. Otis Chandler? ...[20]

He had assumed there would be black representation, and expressed surprise at finding only a single black on the commission.[21]

A foundation executive who did not consider the omission significant, also expressed surprise at the absence of a black female:

... it must have been a gaff ...

Another foundation executive was "not disturbed" by the omission.

A foundation-based professional/intellectual echoed the insignificance of black representation on the commission. And, a foundation executive characterized the group thus:

... it's a balanced commission ...

Several respondents were involved in, or familiar with, the organization of the commission. Their responses suggested a careful and deliberate effort toward composition of its membership:

... there was a political selection mechanism for the commission ... it took three months to assemble it because the members had to meet White House okay ...

... it is under-represented with blacks and females ... they wanted nobody controversial ... tried to avoid people with well-defined stands ... the administration wants to control what happens ...

... there are gaps ... (I) would have selected it differently ... but there is the possibility of supplementing the commission membership with inputs of staff, consultants, and contracts ... where commission is lacking, beef it up with these inputs ...

... there are policy differences: Moynihan advocates accommodating to growth; Finch believes growth can be controlled ... there were differences on the concept of the commission role: Moynihan saw it for forward planning; and Rockefeller saw it to control growth ... policy differences were reflected in process of choosing the Executive Director ...[22]

Again, concerning the specific issue of black representation, a respondent, involved in the composition of the commission asserted:

... (I) didn't want any of that crap ... are there any black demographers? ...

Two respondents, one a professional/intellectual and the other a private influential, expressed reservations about the potential contribution of blacks and poor in a forum such as the commission:

... black representation would be useful only as a potential gimmick ... the poor are inarticulate anyhow, especially in such forums ...

... their wants are known ... they have no organizational capacity ...

A professional/intellectual, who suggested that the role of the commission was principally public realtions-oriented, maintained that the non-represented would be heard:

... (I am) more pleased that enlightened establishment types like Berelson, etc., who can resist the spurious demogogues, are on the commission, than that blacks are not on it ...they can best represent their (black) interests ... [23]

Likewise a private influential observed:

... Beasley has a feel for the five million women ... [24]

An executive of a private association saw the commission as a device for reflecting the attitudes of influential people:

... people who have decided to move themselves ahead ... people who have their own vested interests ...

And so, in reflecting upon the structure within which they operate, the population policy-makers evidence the same pragmatic and non-ideological approach they took in reflecting upon their ultimate purpose, and upon the most effective means of attaining their favorite "visions." There is a basic satisfaction with their apparatus, its composition, its channels of interaction and operating procedures; there is confidence that the structure is compatible with the job to be done. The inadequacies are technocratic; for example, deficiencies in funding, knowledge, and authority, but subject to amelioration by technocratic means. And significant structural alterations are not required for the removal of major obstacles.

Thus, as in the case of ultimate goals and alternative approaches, the actors reflect a noticeable degree of consensus about the quality of their structural arrangements, and little conviction that they might benefit from some re-arrangement.

6 Participatory Policy –Making

A Limited Discourse

The preceding discussion of American population-policy formulation inevitably raises more questions than it answers. This is both of necessity and by design. Of necessity, because the most desirable content of an American population policy is not yet established. All the more reason, then, to define the ingredients of population policy, and then to grapple with all relevant options and choices. By design, because we challenge the inadequate procedures for dealing with American population policy-making. The process requires a more open and searching treatment than it has received in the supposedly wide-open forum of the American political system.

In an earlier chapter, we suggested a concept of population policy which exemplifies the unique characteristic of a population-policy approach in its focus on relationships between aggregates of individuals and the conditions of life available to them. Population-policy formulation is designed to influence these relationships. The objective of American population policy should be to produce opportunities for better conditions of life for any given aggregate of individuals and for society as a whole. Thus population policy is no more than an ingredient of social policy. Accordingly, population policy-making must be pursued within the widest possible framework of social policy-making.

Instead, we find a limited population-policy discourse emphasizing the manipulation of human fertility, and preoccupied with the creation of public policies that will facilitate more effective manipulation of human reproductive behavior. This emphasis has provided the basis for a family-planning strategy which dominates American population-policy efforts both at home and abroad. Thus, a policy discourse is reduced from a more appropriate, though inevitably controversial, social-policy framework to a largely technocratic enterprise. This condition of American population-policy formulation, we suggest, is a consequence of the choices of those involved in making the policy—the American Population Coalition. This Coalition is buttressed by multiple affiliations and relationships among the individuals and institutions involved. And its approach and values, which are reflected in the mobilization of bias operative in its policy-formulation arena, has determined the boundaries within which the discourse takes place. These boundaries are narrow, barring the introduction of positions that might be considered controversial or challenging to the prevailing interpretation of its family-planning theme. Power has been judiciously and skillfully employed to sustain the dominance of the Coalition as the policy-formulation arena dealing with population problems in the United States. And power also has been effectively used to discourage from participating (or otherwise excluding from the discourse) individuals and groups, whether from the mass public or the elite, who do or might express views considered by the Coalition to be deviant.

Whatever their motivations, the Population Coalition has avoided the penetrating issues posed by the ecological commentators (see Chapter 2) which would enrich and enliven the American population-policy discourse. Certainly population specialists are well-equipped to deal with these issues. But such a discussion would include highly controversial matters, such as the reordering and redistribution of advantages, opportunities, and power in American society and abroad. And those involved in population policy-making have demonstrated a preference to exclude these controversial matters from their arena of activity.

Although speculation about the origins of ideological preferences is admittedly a delicate enterprise, the ideological attractiveness of a family-planning strategy to the Population Coalition seems apparent. This strategy envisions the achievement of population limitation in America and abroad, and a corresponding reduction of instability, insecurity and hunger without substantial change in the distribution of power within social and economic institutions. It is an attractive remedy which promises gains without pains, despite the absence of conclusive evidence that family planning by itself is an effective means of reducing fertility and population growth.

Social Policy and Population Policy

The mainstream of scientific evidence demonstrates that choices about fertility are not made in a vacuum, and, frequently, that choices are not made at all because people are not aware that they can be made. The conditions in which people live, their levels of prosperity, education, and knowledge determine fertility choices, or whether fertility choices are made at all. Accordingly, if influencing fertility is a policy objective, then the way to do so is by influencing those conditions within which people live. This relationship suggests the futility of policies attempting direct manipulation of individual fertility performance. Yet, direct manipulation of individual fertility remains the major operational objective of the American Population Coalition.

Even within this restricted interpretation of its policy objective, the Coalition appears to back away from potential controversy. At least two closely-related policy areas are immediately relevant to the success of family planning in the United States alone: one is health care, and the other is population distribution.

Two conditions are required for a successful family-planning enterprise in the

United States—an enterprise designed to provide the opportunity to all Americans to plan families. The first condition is a channel through which the opportunity can be effectively delivered, and the second is an environment in which the opportunity, once available, may be sought and employed by its intended beneficiaries in pursuit of the benefit it is presumed to yield. The absence of either of these conditions renders the opportunity elusive.

At its present stage of development, contraceptive technology is best delivered through a health-care system. The effectiveness of the contraceptive product is dependent upon the ability of the system to make it available to all groups in society, including the poor.

In its existing state, health care in the United States is treated as a commodity subject to trading in the marketplace. This condition subjects it to the elemental forces of the marketplace, the most important of which is a traditional method of allocation involving a pricing mechanism, determined by the interplay of supply and demand. The price of the commodity, and thus its availability, is established by the condition of relative scarcity. The market mechanism may work well in performing a pricing function; but, so long as some are denied access to the marketplace because they have little or nothing to trade, the market mechanism does not work effectively in performing a distribution function.

In a sociological analysis of the medical profession, Freidson argues the failure of consulting professions, including the medical, to: ". . . practice forms of regulation which assure the public that care of uniformly high quality is available to all, irrespective of their economic and social status." This failure is buttressed by a ". . . position of organized autonomy" which provides the profession ". . . its monopoly over special work . . . its special place in the social order . . ." and ". . . permits the profession to create an important segment of the socially-constructed universe."[1] Here, then, is a fundamental constraint upon the capacity of the American health-care enterprise to deliver family-planning opportunity. The population presently denied access to the opportunity is the same population whose access to the marketplace is limited.

The market condition of health care erodes the family-planning opportunity in several respects. Even if contraceptive technology were removed from the market, and allocated by some other mechanism, as American population policy now envisions, other product components, which determine the value of contraceptive technology, remain in the marketplace. Health-care facilities, for example, comprise the points-of-delivery. Yet their existence, capabilities, and geographic distribution are determined largely by the pricing mechanism. Equally critical, and related to the availability and capability of health-care facilities, is the total health-care product available to mothers of living children.[2] The quality of this product is a significant determinant of fertility choices, which the contraceptive technology is supposed to implement. The argument that more healthy and alive mothers and children result in the production of fewer children is made persuasively by Polgar and Kessler. They develop this position in the context of an argument that "family planning and other health services for the family are mutually reinforcing."[3]

Taylor and Hall argue along similar lines: "Increasing evidence shows that health service may be indispensible for reducing population growth. A minimum level of health seems to be necessary for acceptance of the idea and practice of limiting or spacing births. Parents need assurance that children already born will have a reasonable chance for survival. In addition, readily accessible minimum health facilities are probably essential for providing modern contraceptive information and materials."[4]

Siegel has cited the established relationship between the provision of adequate nutrition and the development of intellectual potential, which creates a development syndrome that in itself reduces fertility, i.e., a higher capacity to absorb education leads to improved employment options and opportunities.[5]

Duffy and Cornely have maintained that a modernized concept of health which focuses on the well-being of the family and community is a critical prerequisite for effective family planning.[6] And Duffy has proposed an imaginative strategy to realize the concept.[7]

Yet the total health-care product remains a commodity distributed and priced by exchanges in the marketplace. Until the product, rationally designed to meet community needs, is allocated by a mechanism rationally designed to deliver it to the community, the family-planning opportunity is devalued, and its effectiveness blunted. Accordingly, it is reasonable that those interested in effective family planning might be prompted to take on the system which determines its effectiveness. Flash's analysis of how power is distributed in the American health industry suggests why the Population Coalition might resist the challenge of such a confrontation:

. . . . health providers strongly organized for and occupied with entrepreneurial roles, while held virtually unaccountable politically to society or its governing institutions; . . . health consumers having full (if mythical) recourse to economic sanctions (tradition-hallowed *caveat emptor*), but proscribed from effective political recourse; powerful corporate actors in the health field (commercial insurance companies, non-profit insurance and health-care corporations, nursing home and hospital corporations, medical centers, universities, the Rand Corporation, and survival-hungry problem-transformers from the overwhelming world of aero-space technology) are all welcome at the gaming tables . . . no need to check knives or guns at the door or even to nod at the sheriff on the way in. . . .[8]

While individual fertility preferences are achieved by contraceptive technology, they are largely determined by conditions in the surrounding social and economic environment. These are the conditions that also determine how well individuals are able to live. They comprise the opportunity-package that the community makes available to its members—opportunities for expressing and achieving individual preferences in areas such as education, housing, nutrition, and employment. While these opportunities comprise the objectives that family planning is intended to facilitate, they also determine the value of the family-planning opportunity itself—and, once available, how likely it is to be used by individuals for the achievement of their fertility preferences and as a conduit to a broader range of opportunities.

As presently employed in American population policy, the family-planning formula is designed to influence a single demographic condition—fertility rates. But, for optimal impact, the formula requires an ingredient that would enable it to influence another demographic condition—population distribution.

Like health care, the distribution of population in the United States is not determined by conditions primarily relevant to individual and communal well-being. While the allocation of health care still is influenced by a pricing mechanism, the distribution of the American population, where most of it is concentrated, is influenced in significant measure by bigotry. Thus, residential segregation in metropolitan areas deprives blacks of all opportunities for a better life, including family planning.

Poor whites can choose their place of residence in accordance with their economic capacities, but not blacks. Kain demonstrates that socioeconomic factors do not explain segregation in housing, or the residential distribution of populations in metropolitan areas. Based on his findings, there is a strong justification for the inference that bigotry is a significant determinant of the distribution of the black population.[9] Taueber maintains that it is not necessary to confront the socioeconomic patterns before it is possible to deal with racial residential patterns. Thus, it would be a major accomplishment indeed to reduce racial housing segregation to the level of socioeconomic segregation.[10]

Though it enjoys no juridical status in influencing population distribution, bigotry, camouflaged in juridically acceptable forms ranging from zoning ordinances to ill-disguised manifestations of hostile sentiment, can impede a rational distribution of the American population. Accordingly, the social and economic pathologies resulting from irrational distribution, such as confinement in central cities, are perpetuated, while the social and economic opportunities available through rational distribution are denied. Effective access to the opportunities for freedom of choice in where to live, where to study, where to work, and the like, would create conditions likely to affect fertility behavior by providing an environment which might facilitate the achievement of lower fertility preferences among the population groups where both fertility and deprivation of all opportunities runs highest.

Rational policy approaches to health care and population distribution are likely to achieve multiple benefits. They would round out a limited family-planning formula and open complementary channels to higher levels of individual and communal well-being, which is the announced purpose of the family-planning formula.

But, direct approaches in these areas could require tampering with the existing distribution of political power by antagonizing individuals and groups whose interests and behavior currently bar rational treatment of health care and population dispersal. It is not surprising that the Population Coalition, or any other established policy-making apparatus, might prefer to avoid these formidable obstacles, whatever the merit of so doing.

Numerous reservations have been expressed about the failure to deal with family planning in its broadest social perspective, some by known sympathizers with the family-planning approach. Thus Berelson speculates about the social implications of the traditional planned-parenthood programs:

Are . . . programs themselves a conservative political manifestation, not only in their alleged discriminatory focus upon the lower social classes, but more broadly? . . .[11]

Jaffe calls for a clarification of issues and options, and an assessment of the impact of population-policy alternatives in terms of their political and social consequences in a stratified society.[12] Freymann and associates contend that present value judgments "err toward conservatism," and urge that population policy be developed in a broader conceptual framework aimed at adjusting reproductive patterns to the goal of maximizing the welfare of human groups.[13] Campbell observes that, though family-planning techniques represent a highly efficient channel for easement of economic distress among the poor, they are not a panacea for poverty.[14] Jaffe and Polgar charge that the "culture of poverty" argument is being used by some policy-makers to justify the adoption of measures to coerce reproductive norms.[15]

Rosoff assails the crisis orientation in the population movement and calls for a greater sensitivity to the full range of individual wants:

. . . We should look instead to the variety of ways in which human beings can find independence and self-fulfillment, in which their opportunities are enlarged.[16]

Hilmar warns of the pitfalls to be avoided in evolving a democratic population policy:

. . . one hopes that our very legitimate concern about excessive population growth in the years ahead will not be perverted into propaganda efforts which, by design or by accident, stampede us into willingness and even eagerness to ameliorate our society's population problems by ruthless measures to force down the fertility of the poor, the politically impotent, and the unpopular among us. . . .

. . . If birth control assistance is aggressively pushed on the poor without concurrent and *tangible* efforts to improve their life chances substantially, their "anti-establishment" reactions and suspicions will, with considerable justification, be exacerbated. . . .

. . . If . . . we rely on blatant coercion or "subtle" manipulation to take from couples their options with respect to bearing children, we still cannot guarantee that the birth rate would fall before the government does. And we probably would be embarking on a course of increasingly-brutal oppression which would unduly postpone, if not extinguish, human freedom and responsible self-government. The herd manager and the game warden are not very appealing models to emulate in the management of human affairs.[17]

And Cornely has called for an expanded population policy perspective in the United States. He deplores the narrow interpretation that most frequently leads to a preoccupation with family size and population size, and results in a tendency to talk about population in terms of numbers. He suggests that the population discourse should evolve around a completely different set of referents more relevant to the condition of American society: values, stratification, and racism.[18]

As a result of misgivings for the failure to emplace population-size concerns in a broad social perspective, David and Huang produced an econometric model which would facilitate a systematic evaluation of population change in the context of human and social well-being.[19]

Still, with all the justification for a reordering of priorities away from the traditional fertility strategy, the Population Coalition maintains a traditional family-planning focus. The most recent expression of this position came from the Commission on Population Growth and the American Future. In its report the commission discussed population change in a broad social context, and, indeed, recognized the need for extensive changes in American society. But, having said that American life requires improvement, the commission limited its specific proposals to the area of population growth and fertility control. As for the broader needs, the commission maintained that population growth must decline to buy time for developing the remedies to improve American society.

But if not now, when?

Intellectuals in Policy-Making

By virtue of their access to the policy-making ingredients—knowledge, influence, money, and authority—participants in the Population Coalition are effectively positioned to express their preferences in the policy-making process. Thus they are able to establish a policy arena, monitor its contents and priorities, and exclude conflicting material. As a result of the power they enjoy, this group of policy-makers is able to control population-policy formulation through pre-decision-making and ultimately by non-decision-making. If an expansion of the population-policy discourse were to transpire, the Professional/Intellectual core because of their preeminent role, is in a key position to expand the agenda.

Thus far the results are disappointing. For example, population experts enjoyed the largest sector representation on the Commission for Population

Growth and the American Future. If they tried, they apparently did not succeed in expanding the commission's treatment of population issues beyond a traditional fertility focus.

In the government, the population technocrats are largely responsible for defining research needs, evaluating proposals, and recommending programs. We have observed the fertility/family-planning preference reflected in research activities funded by the Department of HEW and the Agency for International Development, the largest federal funding sources. We have also observed how the "in group" has excluded from its councils some of the dissident voices that are surfacing in the ecological debate. Thus, the existing intellectual and scientific preferences limit broader intellectual and scientific participation in and out of the government.

By exercising the power available to them within the policy-making apparatus the Professional/Intellectuals are able to employ non-decision-making by limiting the intellectual agenda that frames policy choices.

The process of non-decision-making by professionals in the Population Coalition is depicted by Professor Keir Nash, a former Research Director of the Commission on Population Growth and the American Future. He describes an inclination by some prominent intellectual participants in the coalition to limit participation in the discourse by employing a set of values, concepts, and related language which he calls "demographology." This language is the expression of their own intellectual and policy preferences, including the focus on population growth and fertility.

An alternative focus on population distribution is excluded because distribution is "more confounding" and "possibly less manipulable."[20] Nash maintains that this position

suggests another conservative political aspect or thrust to demographology . . . namely the almost fatalistic sense that matters are largely foreordained in respect to population distribution.[21]

But while manipulation of population distribution would be discouraged because of a complicated *status quo*, fertility presents a likely object for manipulation. Nash describes this position as an:

. . . advocacy of an activist position—of bending the political *status quo* to the desired end—when it comes to unwanted fertility. . . . It is tempting to suggest that we are seeing the demographological "shuffle" wherein everyone else's professional subject matter is supposed to change its spots, while one's own leopard skin stays put. . . .
. . . Sometimes it is hard to avoid the conclusion that the logic of demographology constitutes a closed system of reasoning.[22]

The attempt to maintain a preeminent intellectual position influences the character and content of the policy debate. Thus Nash claims:

Freedom of choice—freedom in general—that, I take it, is the crucial value underlying much of the population debate. Of course the question of choice *is* central to the future politics of population if a governmental decision in favor of an explicit and comprehensive population policy is made. But, even now—when the principal political implications of population are those which derive from the fighting of would-be population policy-making outside the population establishment with those inside—it is a strongly motivating word. To put it bluntly, this is why some biologists are so unpopular with some demographers and family planners.[23]

And established intellectual positions, according to Nash, are reinforced by pressures for intellectual orthodoxy which he describes as "the politics of knowledge." Thus, in the population field:

... demographers, and their close "allies" the family planners, have too often overlooked, minimized, or approached with simplistic tools the field's inherent political components. To put it a bit differently, their counting-capacity has hypertrophied while their broad-scale sociopolitical analysis has remained anemic. ... This anemia has been a derivative both of influential demographers' extra-academic policy-desserts and of the powerful reinforcement of the "counting-house" mentality represented by established journals in the field such as *Demography*. One of the most neglected areas of social science study is framed by the question of how a particular discipline's "leading outlets"—and their associated rewards for professors publishing in them—press toward intellectual conformity? Journals in the population field would be a first-class candidate for study for an analyst embarking upon this subarea within the politics of knowledge. ... This establishment network of population journals and experts tends to a conservative policy output.[24]

The restrictive nature of the population coalition is reinforced by the excessive compartmentalization and specialization which characterize scientific pursuits in America. Similar to the behavior of interest groups, which, as Lowi observed, tend not to interfere in areas which do not impinge upon their particular interest, both social and natural scientists, by and large, confine their research and professional interests to their own specialized areas of competence. The consequence of this phenomenon in the population field has been that political, economic, social, and philosophic ramifications of the population problem have been abdicated by social scientists to the expert in population matters—the demographer.[25] But, as a result, the broader issues remain largely unexplored by the population experts.

This defect could be remedied by recruitment and training of diversified expertise in this inherently interdisciplinary field. Population centers affiliated with universities are attempting to correct this deficiency. Although the effort should be applauded, experience in other interdisciplinary subjects, such as urban affairs and areas studies, suggests that differences in methodology and training will not necessarily result in serious challenges to established ideological positions. For example, the Commission on Population Growth and the American Future called upon a wide range of scholars, including the authors, to prepare papers for its consideration. However, there is little indication in its report that the conflicting positions represented in some of these papers broadened the commission's perspective sufficiently to prompt it to raise and grapple with the major issues inherent in the population problem.

We suspect that, in the last analysis, a broadening and vitalization of the population discourse will largely depend upon a greater diversification and democratization of power within the policy-formulating arena. For, widening the range of expertise and ideological diversification in the population research centers alone is not enough. There must be a corresponding ideological diversity among participants in the foundations and institutions which allocate population research funds, and an involvement of mass public participation in public policy-making enterprises, including population policy.

Public Policy and the Comman Man

The illusion needs to be dispelled that scientists and intellectuals live in a world of intellectual objectivity. They and their work increasingly are sought for purposes of policy-making. Policy-making involves political decisions. Accordingly they and their work are politicized, and this reality needs to be known by the intellectuals and scientists, by the consumers of their work, and by the mass public. And however well-known, both within their disciplines and by the public, the increasingly important policy-making role of scientists and intellectuals confers upon them a disproportionate share of power in American political processes.

The traditional institutions of representative government are increasingly remote from the actual processes of policy formulation, as policy-making and its ingredients become more complex. Legislatures frequently legitimize what has been predigested and predecided by the experts. A vote for a legislator thus is an increasingly remote means of registering individual preferences about specific issues. Accordingly, for a meaningful expression of public interest in a context of American representatives democracy, we may require more direct access to the processes of pre-decision-making by more sectors of the American public.

One route is a more direct and easily available access to the technocrats by the mass public. Corporate enterprise, government, foundations and associations can purchase expertise in a market they largely control. We have seen some of these linkages in the population field. But mass publics are deprived of recourse to expertise, largely for organizational and economic reasons. There is no systematic method for mass publics to enlist the aid of experts in articulating and expressing their concerns. And there is little perceptible inclination by the technocrats to expose their findings and recommendations to amorphous groups in the American mass public.

Nobody asked the poor females of America how they want their family-planning packaged—whether as opportunities for more education, better maternal/child-care facilities, a network of day-care facilities, or family-planning clinics. The decisions were made for them by persons confident of *their* judgment in such matters, the technocrats. Unless the experts take the initiative in rallying mass publics in matters such as automotive safety, flammable fabrics, deceptive packaging, and the like, the mass public concern remains submerged by the complicated policy-making machinery that only experts know how to manipulate. And few experts take the initiative in communicating with mass publics, not necessarily for lack of compassion or because of dereliction of their civic responsibility, but because professional rewards do not accrue from taking such initiatives. Thus it is a legitimate function of our political system to establish mechanisms for public access to the experts.

In the population field, for example, public members could be included on the government advisory boards that evaluate program initiatives, and the research proposals upon which they are based. At present the research panels at the National Institutes of Health and the Research Advisory Committee of the Agency for International Development are composed exclusively of scientists and intellectuals. These are the bodies that effectively determine U.S. government research strategies, and thus shape policy agendas, in the population field. They lack public representation that might raise questions about the relevance and responsiveness of the strategies and agendas to the variety of public concerns and anxieties.

It could be said that laymen never would comprehend a research proposal. But, if so, as it often is among laymen and experts alike, this failure reflects the deficiency of the proposal more than the intelligence and sensitivity of the laymen. So long as research proposals are relevant to public policy-making, they must be sufficiently comprehensible to allow for a modicum of public evaluation. Otherwise the choices that inevitably are involved in, and emerge from, the research are predetermined by technocrats on behalf of the public. And thus technocratic power is employed to limit public choice.

And beyond the systematic linkage of technocrat and mass public, there is the issue of greater participation by concerned publics within the full spectrum of policy formulation, especially when it affects them. Here again there is a great deal of modern-day noblesse oblige, of patronizing, of speaking on behalf of the policy consumer by self-appointed policy producers who are confident of their judgments about the requirements of the consumers. But how often is the potential consumer of the remedies, including population remedies, asked to rank his order of choices about the alternatives?

In this connection, we should reflect on the absence from the population-policy machinery of the principal policy consumers—the poor, the blacks, the other minority groups, and the females. Some have argued that their wants are known, that they are ineffective spokesmen on their own behalf, and that their interests are effectively represented by others. The credibility of this argument, for which supporting evidence is absent, is doubtful. It has been argued that responsive and responsible policy-making does not require the direct involvement in the policy-making process of the consumers of policy remedies, the beneficiaries of policy allocations, and the constituencies of policy areas. This argument too lacks substantiation.

Examples of the central involvement of beneficiaries, or their representatives, and their influence in shaping public policy in the areas in which they have a direct interest are not hard to come by. The maritime, aviation, railroad, and trucking industries are involved in federal support and regulation of transportation; electricity producers and electric cooperatives in utilities regulation; farmers in farm policy; veterans in veterans' benefits; members of trade unions in labor policy. Their inputs are made from institutional bases created specifically in response to opportunities for direct participation in policy-making—trade associations, farm groups, veterans' organizations, labor political action groups, and the like.

The population-policy process differs, since the principal beneficiaries of population policy are uniformly *non*-participants in the policy-making that directly affects them, and conversely, those who participate in policy-making in this area are uniformly *non*-beneficiaries.

To some degree these contrasting phenomena are not difficult to understand. The target populations—predominantly poor, black, and urban women and their spouses—are poorly organized and unequipped to participate in shaping policy through any of the established channels. They are not aware of the significance, or even existence, of congressional hearings on population, and the commissions and panels, let alone the population discourse. However, and most important, neither the leaders within the Population Coalition nor those who organize recognized policy-making forums have indicated more than passing and symbolic gestures to involve mass public participation in the policy-making process.

Leaders in the Coalition claim to be dedicated to providing greater freedom and opportunity for mass publics in America and throughout the world. There is no reason to question their sincerity. However, the upper-class character of the Coalition suggests the presence of another motive which might affect some of them: a desire to secure a future in which their own privileged positions and life-styles will be preserved. To the extent this kind of concern is present—consciously or unconsciously—among Coalition leaders, the contrast we have made between the Population Coalition and other interest group subsystems (labor, veterans, business, etc.) does *not* actually exist; for, many of the primary beneficiaries of the Population Coalition's product are—similar to the pattern of other interest groups—very much *within* not outside, the Coalition. Moreover, and again like other policy arenas, the interests of elites within the Population Coalition are potentially in sharp conflict with the unorganized beneficiaries who are outside of the policy-making system.

Of course, elites in the Coalition are genuinely interested in supporting and working for measures that will result in greater freedom and opportunity for ordinary people. But their commitment to this goal is circumscribed within safe political bounds. It would be fanciful, for example, to conceive of the Hugh Moore group, which publishes the strident advertisements calling for birth control, supporting equally energetic appeals for the immediate dispersal of ghetto populations in the suburbs of metropolitan areas.[26] And it would be unlikely to find full-page *New York Times* advertisements sponsored by this impressive group of Americans pleading for a rational health-care system that would serve the needs of all Americans. Yet, a more rational deployment of population and a more responsive health-care system are likely to be more effective routes to fertility control than a limited family-planning strategy.

Likewise, it would be unreasonable to expect the influential Population Crisis Committee, with its "Fortune 500" profile, to support an effective suburban population dispersal strategy, or a rational health care strategy, or an equal educational and job opportunity strategy for women with the same vigor and skill they have devoted to the cause of fertility control. Even the good citizens who have supported voluntary family planning through the national network of Planned Parenthood affiliates could not reasonably be expected to coalesce around an expanded ideology that would, for instance, lead to the enforcement of the rights of all Americans to live where they prefer. Nor could they be expected to endorse Maurice Strong's belief that a viable policy to combat the deterioration of the planet's life-supporting systems requires the rich, the privileged, and the well-born to radically change—if not revolutionize—their attitudes and values. The strategy which the Coalition has embraced in its family-planning formula is, in short, one that reduces the area of potential controversy to issues that are familiar, task-oriented, and congenial to existing political and social structures. Thus, the existing policy-making structure limits the choices.

An open and democratic process for formulating population policy requires more direct participation from at least three groups—racial minorities, women, an expanded core of scientists and intellectuals, and even the Archie Bunkers of left as well as right. So long as the "population problem" remains a circumscribed and discrete subject, neither will the professionals within the Coalition be threatened by "foreign" consideration and expertise, nor will their colleagues within the foundations and population-interest groups be confronted by "extraneous" social and political issues. Together they can remain undisturbed to move ahead in providing contraceptive technology and services, as they determine the need.

It is unlikely that the restrictive nature of the population policy arena is unique in American politics. Other policy areas which rely heavily upon a core of experts who work closely with other elite groups—such as national defense, space, mental health, pollution abatement, and the like—may well manifest the same characteristics as the Population Coalition. It could well be that the growth in technology has rendered our traditional form of representative government inadequate for democratic policy-making in an increasing number of vital areas. If so, we should proceed vigorously to modernize a venerable system whose growing obsolescence could cost us dearly. And the relatively new population-policy area may well provide some clues as to how we should proceed.

Notes

Notes

Chapter 1
A Power Approach to Policy Formulation

1. The significance of these reciprocal relationships between aggregates of people has been articulated by Goldscheider:

. . . the cumulative processes of population events and the resultant implications for the size, distribution, and composition of populations are fundamental to the structure and functioning of human societies. People are the stuff from which families, groups, societies and nations are constructed; the processes of population are the building blocks shaping the form and content of social units. In turn, the individual and personal aspects of population phenomena are conditioned and affected by the power of social forces; what appears on the surface to represent biological and idiosyncratic events are by their nature social as well.

. . . The size, growth, density, concentration of population, birth and death rates, cityward and suburbanward migrations, have become social issues for many reasons and in various social contexts, but mainly because population processes affect and are affected by the organization and anatomy of society. The quantity of population shapes the quality of social life. The reverse is equally true; the quality and fabric of social life shape the quantity and character of population processes. Calvin Goldscheider, POPULATION, MODERNIZATION, AND SOCIAL STRUCTURE, Boston: Little Brown & Co., 1971. pp. 3-4.

The potential for influencing these relationships, which is population policy-making, might be depicted as follows:

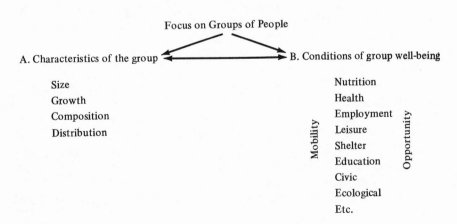

Population policy influences the reciprocal relationships between "A" and "B"

Figure N-1. Perspective for Population Policy-making

2. Robert Dahl, "The Concept of Power," BEHAVIORAL SCIENCES, 2 (1957) p. 202.

3. This definition is partially drawn from Kenneth M. Dolbeare and Murray J. Edelman, AMERICAN POLITICS: POLITICS, POWER AND CHANGE, Lexington, Mass.: D.C. Heath and Co., 1971, p. 57.

4. Robert Dahl, WHO GOVERNS?, New Haven: Yale University Press, 1961; Edward C. Banfield, POLITICAL INFLUENCE, New York: Free Press, 1961; and Nelson Polsby, COMMUNITY POWER AND POLITICAL THEORY, New Haven: Yale University Press, 1963.

5. Peter Bachrach and Morton S. Baratz, POWER AND POVERTY, New York: Oxford University Press, 1970.

6. This paragraph is an extrapolation from E.E. Schattschneider's discussion of the contagiousness of conflict. See his THE SEMISOVEREIGN PEOPLE, New York: Holt, Rinehart, and Winston, 1960, Chapter 1.

7. The "old boy network" is a creature of British political culture. It refers to the alright types who are born to good families, attend the right schools, belong to the same clubs, and as a predictable result tend to run into each other in their assorted social, professional, civic, and martial pursuits. In the past they also tended to run England. The most common American counterpart is a phenomenon some describe and some deplore as the "Eastern establishment." There could be a spillover of this phenomenon in the Population Coalition. At least one interview respondent described it in a nonpejorative sense as a "rich man's club."

8. Op. cit., Schattschneider.

9. Jack Walker, "A Critique of the Elitist Theory of Democracy," AMERICAN POLITICAL SCIENCE REVIEW, 60, 1966, p. 288.

10. For an interesting discussion of this problem, see Roger W. Cobb and Charles D. Elder, PARTICIPATION IN AMERICAN POLITICS: THE DYNAMICS OF AGENDA-BUILDING, Boston: Allyn and Bacon, 1972.

11. Theodore J. Lowi, THE END OF LIBERALISM, New York: W.W. Norton, 1969.

12. For a discussion of other forms of non-decision-making, see Bachrach and Baratz, op. cit., Chapter 3.

13. See Richard M. Merelman, "Nondecisions and the Study of Local Politics," AMERICAN POLITICAL SCIENCE REVIEW, 65 (1971) pp. 1063-1104, and Raymond Wolfinger, "On the Neo-Elitist Critique of Community Power," AMERICAN POLITICAL SCIENCE REVIEW, LXII, 1968, pp. 451-61. For an excellent radical critique of this concept, see Isaac Balbus, "The Concept of Interest in Pluralist and Marxist Analysis," POLITICS AND SOCIETY, 1, 1971, pp. 161-177.

14. Cobb and Elder, op. cit., p. 12.

15. James B. Rule, "The Problem with Social Problems," POLITICS AND SOCIETY, 11 (1971), p. 48.

Chapter 2
The Politicization of Ecology

1. Thomas Malthus, THE FIRST ESSAY (Paperback ed.), Ann Arbor: University of Michigan Press, 1959, pp. 4-5.

2. Roger Revelle, Book Review of Paul Ehrlich and Ann Ehrlich, POPULATION, RESOURCES, ENVIRONMENT: ISSUES IN HUMAN ECOLOGY, IN FAMILY PERSPECTIVES 3, Vol. 2, 1971, p. 66.

3. Public Law 91-572, 91st Cong., 2d Sess.

4. For a statement of this position, see: Frederick S. Jaffe and Steven P. Polgar, "Family Planning and Public Policy: Is the 'Culture of Poverty' the New Cop-Out?" JOURNAL OF MARRIAGE AND THE FAMILY, May 1968.

5. See, for example: Philip M. Hauser, "Family Planning and Population Programs," DEMOGRAPHY, vol. 4, pt. 1, 1967. pp. 397-414.

6. This position is reflected in the policy recommendations of the National Academy of Sciences Study Committee. See Study Committee of the Office of the Foreign Secretary, National Academy of Sciences, RAPID POPULATION GROWTH: CONSEQUENCES AND POLICY IMPLICATIONS, Baltimore: The Johns Hopkins Press, 1971.

7. Garrett J. Hardin, "The Tragedy of the Commons," SCIENCE, December 13, 1968. 162: 1243-1248.

8. Ibid.

9. The antinatalist proposals, among others, are comprehensively inventoried in Bernard Berelson, "Beyond Family Planning," STUDIES IN FAMILY PLANNING, vol. 38, February 1969.

10. Samuel McCracken, "The Population Controller," COMMENTARY, vol. 53, no. 5, 1972, p. 48.

11. Barry Commoner, THE CLOSING CIRCLE; NATURE, MAN AND TECHNOLOGY, N.Y., Knopf, 1971; Paul Ehrlich and Ann H. Ehrlich, POPULATION, RESOURCES AND ENVIRONMENT: ISSUES IN HUMAN ECOLOGY, San Francisco: W.H. Freeman and Company, 1970; and Donella H. Meadows, Dennis L. Meadows, Jorgen Randers and William W. Behrens III, THE LIMITS OF GROWTH, New York: University Books, 1972.

12. Philip M. Hauser, "Review of Ehrlich, Paul R. and Anne H. Population, Resources, Environment: Issues in Human Ecology," SOCIAL BIOLOGY, Dec. 1971, pp. 443-446.

13. Norman Cousins, "New York's Fight Against Pollution," SATURDAY REVIEW, March 7, 1970, p. 53-54.

14. Op. cit., Ehrlich, p. 300

15. Ibid., p. 323.

16. Barry Commoner, "Motherhood in Stockholm," HARPERS MAGAZINE, 244, June 1972, p. 50.

17. Op. cit., Ehrlich, p. 300.

18. Op. cit., Commoner, p. 50.

19. Op. cit., Ehrlich, p. 300.

20. Ibid., p. 302.

21. Op. cit., Commoner et al., Closing Circle.

22. Review of THE CLOSING CIRCLE in Environment 14, no. 3, 1972, p. 25.

23. Barry Commoner, "The Environmental Cost of Economic Growth," CHEMISTRY IN BRITAIN Vol. 8, no. 2, Feb. 1972, pp. 52-65.

24. Ibid., p. 51.

25. Ibid., p. 37.

26. Ibid., p. 52.

27. Ibid., p. 51.

28. Op. cit., Commoner et al., Limits of Growth.

29. Ibid., pp. 161-163.

30. Ibid., pp. 165-166.

31. Peter Passell, Marc Roberts and Leonard Ross, Review of THE LIMITS OF GROWTH, in THE NEW YORK TIMES BOOK REVIEW, April 2, 1972, p. 12.

32. Op. cit., Commoner et al. LIMITS OF GROWTH, pp. 132-133.

33. Ibid., pp. 140-141.

34. Ibid., p. 150.

35. Ibid., p. 145.

36. Ibid., p. 53.

37. Quoted in Ibid., p. 179.

38. NEW YORK TIMES, May 7, 1972, p. 29.

39. Quoted in Commoner, p. 50.

40. Ahmed Bahri, Maaza Bekele, Anita Bensaid, Olivier le Brun, et. al., A NEW APPROACH TO POPULATION RESEARCH IN AFRICA: IDEOLOGIES, FACTS AND POLITICS, Unpublished, December 1971, p. 5.

41. Ibid., p. 5.

42. Ibid., p. 6.

43. Ibid., pp. 5-9.

44. J. Mayone Stycos, "Opinion, Ideology, and Population Problems—Some Sources of Domestic and Foreign Opposition to Birth Control," in NATIONAL ACADEMY volume, op. cit., pp. 533-566.

45. Ibid.

46. Ibid.

47. From statement of Reverend Jesse Jackson reported in unpublished Summary of Public Hearings held by the Commission in Washington, Los Angeles, Chicago and Little Rock, Commission on Population Growth and the American Future, Washington, D.C., 1971.

48. Neil Chamberlain, BEYOND MALTHUS: POPULATION AND POWER, New York: Basic Books, 1970, pp. 45-49.

49. For example, see Jerome Skolnick, POLITICS OF PROTEST, New York, Ballentine Books, 1970.

50. Roger Revelle, "The Population Dilemma People and Behavior," Harvard University, Center for Population Studies, Contribution No. 65. Reprinted from PSYCHIATRIC ANNALS, I, 1, Sept. 1971.

51. Commoner et al. Closing Circle, p. 243.

52. Op. cit., Revelle, Book Review, p. 67.

53. Ibid., p. 68.

54. Ibid., p. 67.

55. Gladwin Hill, "Draft Calls for Ecological Responsibility," NEW YORK TIMES, June 7, 1972, p. 16.

56. Anthony Lewis, "Growth and Politics," NEW YORK TIMES, June 18, 1972.

57. Kingsley Davis, "Population Policy: Will Current Programs Succeed?," SCIENCE, November 10, 1967, pp. 730-739.

58. Rudolph Klein, "Growth and Its Enemies," COMMENTARY, June, 1972, pp. 37-44.

59. Op. cit., Commoner et al., LIMITS OF GROWTH.

60. See The Report of the Commission on Population Growth & American Future, POPULATION AND THE AMERICAN FUTURE, New York: New American Library, 1972.

61. Ibid.

62. NEW YORK TIMES, April 30, 1972, Sect. 12.

63. NEW YORK TIMES, May 6, 1972, pp. 1, 8.

64. Ibid.

65. Ibid.

66. Op. cit., Commission, p. 3.

67. Ibid., p. 172.

68. Ibid., pp. 2, 7, 149.

69. Ibid., p. 170.

70. Ibid., p. 178.

71. NEW YORK TIMES, May 6, 1972, pp. 1, 8.

72. Op. cit., Commission, p. 4.

73. Ibid., p. 7, 117.

74. Ibid., pp. 45-53.

75. Op. cit., Commission.

76. See Commissioner Otis Duncan's separate statement on this subject, see Commission, pp. 274-275.

77. Op. cit., Commission, pp. 70, 57.

78. Op. cit., Commoner et al., Closing Circle and Cousins.

79. Op. cit., Commission, p. 75.

80. Op. cit., Commission.

81. NEW YORK TIMES, June 11, 1972. (Italics ours.)

82. Op. cit., Commission (Italics ours.)
83. Ibid.
84. Ibid.
85. Ibid.
86. Ibid.
87. Ibid.
88. Ibid.

Chapter 3
Beyond Family Planning

1. Bernard Berelson, "Beyond Family Planning," STUDIES IN FAMILY PLANNING, vol. 38, February, 1969, pp. 1-16.

2. Ibid., p. 3.

3. Ibid.

4. Ibid., p. 1.

5. Cuban demographers have reported a drop in the population growth rate from 2.5 to 2.0 during the 1960-1970 decade. (See report by Juan de Onis in NEW YORK TIMES, January 6, 1971.) It is possible that this phenomenon is not explained exclusively by the large-scale emigration of the 60s.

For further discussion of the 1970 Cuban census including an observation of declining fertility, see also Jacques Houdaille, "Premier Resultats du Recensement de Cuba," POPULATION, May-June, 1971, pp. 589-590.

6. Berelson, op. cit., p. 6.

7. Ibid. (Emphasis ours.)

8. Ibid., p. 8.

9. The significance of these structural alternatives in mediating attitudes and behavior, and the failure of the family-planning advocates to deal with them satisfactorily, is discussed, among other places, in: Benedict J. Duffy, Jr. and Paul B. Cornely, "Beyond Birth Control to Family Services and Family Planning," (Paper prepared for the 12th Congress of the International Federation of Catholic Medical Associations, Shoreham Hotel, Washington, D.C., October 11-14, 1970), and R. Kenneth Godwin, "The Structure of Mass Attitudes Toward Family Planning and Family Size: The Implications for Policy." (Forthcoming)

10. Tillman Durdin, "China's Changing Society Seems to Cut Birth Rate," NEW YORK TIMES, April 21, 1971, p. 1; Edgar Snow, "China: Population Care and Control," NEW REPUBLIC, May 1, 1971, pp. 20-23; Seymour Topping, "China: Economic Policy Stresses Local Self-Help," NEW YORK TIMES, June 27, 1971, p. 1.

11. Berelson, op. cit., p. 12.

12. Berelson, "Population Policy: Personal Notes," POPULATION STUDIES vol. 25, no. 2, 1971, pp. 173-182.

13. Kingsley Davis, "Population Policy: Will Current Programs Succeed?" SCIENCE, 10 November 1967, pp. 158, 730-739.

14. Letters from Committee on Population, National Academy of Sciences, and Kingsley Davis "Family Planning and Other Population Controls" (Published in SCIENCE, February 23, 1968), p. 827-829. (Emphasis ours.)

15. Ibid., p. 829.

16. Ibid.

17. Frederick S. Jaffe, "Man's Relationship to the Environment as Influenced by Overpopulation" (Address at the Symposium, University of New Hampshire, September 25, 1969).

18. Quoted by R.T. Ravenholt and J.J. Speidel, "Prostaglandins in Family-Planning Strategy" (Paper presented at the Conference on Prostaglandins, New York Academy of Sciences, New York, September 19, 1970), p. 3. (Emphasis ours.)

Chapter 4
The Anatomy of a Coalition

1. The Rockefeller Foundation. PRESIDENT'S TEN-YEAR REVIEW AND ANNUAL REPORT 1971.

2. The evolution of the Planned Parenthood Movement in the United States is best recorded and evaluated in: David M. Kennedy BIRTH CONTROL IN AMERICA: THE CAREER OF MARGARET SANGER, New Haven: Yale University Press, 1970. (Note particularly the comprehensive bibliographical essay.) See also the review of this volume: Alan F. Guttmacher "Margaret Sanger's New Look," FAMILY PLANNING PERSPECTIVES, vol. 2, no. 3, June 1970, pp. 49-50.

3. A chronology of the development of research and teaching activities is provided in an unpublished paper by Deborah Oakley, "A History and Analysis of U.S. Governmental Efforts in Population Research, 1969-1971," Center for Population Planning, University of Michigan, September 1971.

4. From an unpublished Population Council memorandum.

5. Figure derived from the financial data in the Annual Reports of the Population Council, covering the period 1952-1970.

6. Population Association of America, "Directory of Population Study Centers, United States and Canada, 1971."

7. Detailed information on these enterprises is best reflected in the annual reports of The Ford Foundation, The Rockefeller Foundation, The Population Council, and in the annual INVENTORY OF POPULATION RESEARCH SUPPORTED BY FEDERAL AGENCIES.

8. Lawrence Lader, BREEDING OURSELVES TO DEATH, New York: Ballentine Books, 1971, p. 1.

9. Ibid.

10. Ibid., p. 7.

11. An analysis of the distribution of the Population Crisis Committee membership is reflected in Elihu Bergman, THE POLITICS OF POPULATION USA: A CRITIQUE OF THE POLICY PROCESS, Population Program and Policy Design Series, no. 5. Chapel Hill: Carolina Population Center, 1972, pp. 93-95.

12. ZPG NATIONAL REPORTER, March 1972, p. 2.

13. Characterization volunteered by an official of Planned Parenthood/World Population.

14. See replica of advertisement on page 48.

15. U.S. President's Committee to Study the United States' Military Assistance Program, composite report, Washington, D.C., 1959.

16. Op. cit., unpublished paper by Deborah Oakley.

17. Ibid.

18. Ibid.

19. Agency for International Development, Washington, D.C. POPULATION PROGRAM ASSISTANCE, December, 1971.

20. This group was called The Committee on Resources and Man, of The National Academy of Sciences/National Research Council.

21. A Consultants' Report by Oscar Harkavy, Frederick S. Jaffe, and Samuel M. Wishik, "Implementing DHEW Policy on Family Planning and Population," September, 1967.

22. A single volume summary of these hearings is available as POPULATION CRISIS, Washington: Socio-Dynamic Publications, 1970.

23. For a detailed identification of these hearings, see Bergman, op. cit., pp. 43-62.

24. Ibid., pp. 80-84.

25. Bernard Berelson, "Beyond Family Planning" STUDIES IN FAMILY PLANNING, no. 38, February 1969, pp. 1-16.

26. The identification of the individuals and their institutions is available in Bergman, op. cit., pp. 72-74.

27. Source: The Population Council of America, Annual Reports 1956-1970.

28. Ibid., also THE POPULATION COUNCIL 1952-1964, A REPORT: JULY 1965: and THE POPULATION COUNCIL, INC. REPORTS OF THE EXECUTIVE OFFICERS FOR THE PERIOD NOVEMBER 5, 1952 to DECEMBER 31, 1955.

29. The Ford Foundation, SUMMARY OF GRANTS AND FOUNDATION-ADMINISTERED PROJECTS IN POPULATION AND FAMILY PLANNING, TO OCTOBER 1, 1971.

30. POPULATION RESEARCH, THE FEDERAL PROGRAM, INVENTORY OF POPULATION RESEARCH SUPPORTED BY FEDERAL AGENCIES, FISCAL YEAR 1971, PREPARED FOR THE INTERAGENCY COMMITTEE ON POPULATION RESEARCH, DHEW PUBLICATION (NIH), no. 72-133.

31. AID, POPULATION PROGRAM ASSISTANCE, op. cit.

Chapter 5
Reflections of a Coalition

1. The term "discussion" is used to embrace several sessions not conducted as formal interviews, but in which the purpose of this inquiry was described, and questions were raised which related directly to it. Some of these sessions yielded valuable information, and those that did are included in the "data base."

2. As excellent references for how to "zero in" on influentials, see Robert Presthus, MEN AT THE TOP: A STUDY IN COMMUNITY POWER, New York: Oxford University Press, 1964, and Kenneth Gergen "Assessing the Leverage Points" in R.A. Bauer and Kenneth Gergen (eds.), THE STUDY OF POLICY FORMATION, New York: The Free Press, 1968.

3. The respondents were affiliated with the following institutions: The Ford Foundation, The Rockefeller Foundation, The Population Council, Planned Parenthood-World Population Center for Family Planning Program Development, International Planned Parenthood Federation (The Victor-Bostrom Fund), Population Crisis Committee, The University of Chicago, the University of North Carolina, U.S. Senate, U.S. House of Representatives, the Bureau of the Census, the Department of State (Agency for International Development), Commission on Population Growth and the American Future, Department of Health, Education and Welfare (Office of Deputy Assistant Secretary for Population Affairs, National Institute of Child Health and Human Development, Center for Population Research), Office of Economic Opportunity, the White House.

4. In support of this approach see Lewis Dexter, ELITE AND SPECIALIZED INTERVIEWING, Evanston: Northwestern University Press, 1970.

5. Both Congressmen were among the most active in population legislation during the 91st Congress.

6. These reactions typify an increasing concern for the consequences of piggybacking eco-environmental issues on population issues, and thereby distorting the nature of the population issues. This piggybacking, which has created something of a middle-class crusade is popularized in full-page newspaper advertisements sponsored by the Hugh Moore Fund in THE NEW YORK TIMES, September 27, 1970, Sect. E, p. 7, and by Paul Ehrlich's paperback bestseller, THE POPULATION BOMB, New York: Ballantine, 1964. See Professor Philip Hauser's warning about the consequences of these distortions in Chapter 2, p. 15.

In an expanded version of his argument, Hauser dismantles eight propositions (he calls them "distortions") that comprise the ideological core of the environmentalist position. See Philip M. Hauser, "On Population and Environmental Policy and Problem" (Paper prepared from transcription of extemporaneous talk at the First National Congress on Optimum Population and the Environment at the Pick-Congress Hotel, Chicago, June 8, 1970).

Another treatment of the eco-environmental doomsday position is presented in, Ben J. Wattenberg, "The Nonsense Explosion," NEW REPUBLIC, April 4, 1970, pp. 18-23, May 9, 1970, pp. 46-47.

7. Actually the organization in question manages to function with eclectic norms. One unit bases its activities on a "birth control" objective, while another claims "human welfare" as the grounds for its work.

8. The meeting referred to was the International Conference on Family Planning Programs at Geneva, Switzerland, August 23-27, 1965. It was sponsored by the Ford Foundation, Population Council, and Rockefeller Foundation, and attended by nearly 200 participants from 36 countries. The Conference proceedings appear in Bernard Berelson, et al. (eds.), FAMILY PLANNING AND POPULATION PROGRAMS, Chicago: University of Chicago Press, 1965.

The challenge appeared in a review of the proceedings: Philip M. Hauser, "Family Planning and Population Programs," DEMOGRAPHY, vol. 4, pt. 1, 1967, p. 414.

9. Carl Flemister, "Population Control and the Black Revolution" (Address presented to the Population Seminar, Carolina Population Center, Chapel Hill, March 23, 1970).

10. Charles Arnold and Philip Hauser, contributions in "Needed Research on Demographic Aspects of the Black Community," THE MILBANK MEMORIAL FUND QUARTERLY, vol. XLVIII, no. 2, pt. 2, April 1970.

11. Barry Commoner, "Survival in the Environmental-Population Crisis" (Paper presented at the Annual Meeting of the American Association for the Advancement of Science, Boston, December 29, 1969).

12. T. Paul Schultz, "Population Growth and Internal Migration in Colombia," Memorandum RM-5765-RC/AID, The Rand Corporation, Santa Monica, July, 1969.

13. Marc Nerove and T. Paul Schultz, "Love and Life Between the Censuses: A Model of Family Decision Making in Puerto Rico, 1950-1960," RM-6322-AID, The Rand Corporation, Santa Monica, September, 1970.

14. Simon S. Kuznets, "Economic Aspects of Fertility Rates in the Less Developed Countries," in S.J. Behrman, Leslie Corsa, and Ronald Freedman, ed., FERTILITY AND FAMILY PLANNING: A WORLD VIEW, Ann Arbor: The University of Michigan Press, 1970, pp. 157-179.

15. The functions and membership of the Commission on Population Growth and the American Future was described in Chapter 4.

16. General William F. Draper, Jr., described in Chapter 4.

17. The particular Draper organization referred to is the Population Crisis Committee. (See Chapter 4.)

18. A clarification of organizational terminology: the reference to IPPF was intended to mean its U.S. affiliate—Planned Parenthood—World Population. The National Institution of Child Health and Human Development (NICHD) is the organizational location of the Center for Population Research.

19. See presidential message to the Congress on Population, July 18, 1969, and Family Planning Services and Population Research Act of 1970.

20. Mrs. Otis Chandler is the white spouse of the publisher of the LOS ANGELES TIMES.

21. The black member is Dr. Paul Cornely of Howard University, then President of the American Public Health Association. (Two more blocks were subsequently added as replacements for original appointees.)

22. The reference is to Robert Finch, then Secretary of Health, Education and Welfare, and Daniel Patrick Moynihan, then Counselor to the President, who was the White House functionary most closely involved with creation of the Commission.

23. The reference is to Bernard Berelson, President of the Population Council.

24. The reference is to Dr. Joseph Beasley, Director of the statewide family-planning program in Louisiana, and the five million American females requiring subsidized family-planning services.

Chapter 6
Participatory Policy-Making

1. Eliot Friedson, PROFESSION OF MEDICINE: A STUDY OF THE SOCIOLOGY OF APPLIED KNOWLEDGE, New York: Dodd, Mead & Company, 1970, pp. 378-379. In addition to a segment of the socially-constructed universe, the condition of "organized autonomy" also facilitates a form of oligopolistic control over a segment of the marketplace; in this case, that corner where medical care is traded. This restrictive condition prevents distribution of the product without regard to economic and social status.

See also an indictment of the American health-care system for failing to serve its constituency, i.e., all Americans who require health care, John and Barbara Ehrenreich, THE AMERICAN HEALTH CARE EMPIRE. A REPORT FROM THE HEALTH POLICY ADVISORY CENTER, New York: Random House, 1971.

2. The requirement for an adequate health care system to achieve both fertility reduction and better society goals is argued for, among others, by Harald Frederiksen, "Feedbacks in Economic and Demographic Transition," SCIENCE, vol. 166, November 14, 1969; Steven Polgar, "Population History and Population Policy From An Anthropological Perspective," CURRENT ANTHROPOLOGY, Vol. 13, April 1972, pp. 203-211.

3. Steven Polgar and Alexander Kessler, AN INTRODUCTION TO FAMILY PLANNING IN THE CONTEXT OF HEALTH SERVICES, (Geneva: World Health Organization, August 1968).

4. Carl E. Taylor and Marie-Francoise Hall, "Health, Population, and Economic Development," SCIENCE, August 11, 1967, pp. 651-657.

5. "Topical Investigation and Analysis of Promoting Family Planning Through Health Services," Population Planning and Statistics Series, Research Triangle Institute, Research Triangle Park, North Carolina, 1970, p. 12.

6. Benedict J. Duffy, Jr., and Paul B. Cornely, "Beyond Birth Control to Family Services and Family Planning (Paper prepared for the 12th Congress of the International Federation of Catholic Medical Associations, Washington, D.C., October 11-14, 1970).

7. Benedict J. Duffy, Jr., "Consumers, Cities, and Health," (Statement for Boston meeting on the President's Committee on Health Education, January 6, 1972).

8. William S. Flash, "Political Implications of National Health Insurance Proposals" (Paper prepared for presentation at the Conference of Social Behavioral Sciences in Health and the Medical Care Section, American Public Health Association, Houston, October 25, 1970).

9. John F. Kain, ed., RACE AND POVERTY: THE ECONOMICS OF DISCRIMINATION, Englewood Cliffs: Prentice-Hall, 1969, pp. 22-27.

10. Karl E. Taueber, "Negro Population and Housing: Demographic Aspects of a Social Accounting Scheme" in Irwin Katz and Patricia Gurin, eds., RACE AND THE SOCIAL SCIENCES, New York: Basic Books, 1969, pp. 145-194.

11. Bernard Berelson, "Population Policy: Current Issues" (Address to Population Association of America Meeting, April 10, 1969).

12. Frederick S. Jaffe, "Activities Relevant to the Study of Population Policy in the United States," Memorandum to Bernard Berelson, February 13, 1969.

13. Moye W. Freymann, ed., APPROACHES TO THE HUMAN FERTILITY PROBLEM, Chapel Hill: Carolina Population Center, 1968.

14. Arthur A. Campbell, "The Role of Family Planning in the Reduction of Poverty," JOURNAL OF MARRIAGE AND THE FAMILY, vol. 30, no. 2, May 1968, pp. 236-245.

15. Frederick S. Jaffe and Steven P. Polgar, "Family Planning and Public Policy: Is the 'Culture of Poverty' the New Cop-Out?," JOURNAL OF MARRIAGE AND THE FAMILY, vol. 30, no. 2, May 1968, 228-235.

16. Jeannie I. Rosoff, "Crisis Thinking—Rhetoric vs. Action," FAMILY PLANNING PERSPECTIVES, vol. 2, no. 3, June 1970, pp. 27-29.

17. Norman A. Hilmar, "Population Control, Family Planning and Planned Parenthood" (Address presented at Planned Parenthood-World Population Southeast Council/National Board Meeting, Savannah, Georgia, May 7, 1970).

18. Paul B. Cornely, The Third Annual Fred T. Foard Jr. Memorial Lecture, The School of Public Health, The University of North Carolina at Chapel Hill, February 11, 1971.

19. Abraham S. David and Ching-Ju Huang, "Population Theory and the Concept of Optimum Population," SOCIO-ECONOMIC PLANNING SCIENCE, vol. 3, 1969, pp. 191-217.

20. A. E. Keir Nash, "Demographology in U.S. Population Politics," in R.L. Clinton and W.K. Godwin, eds., RESEARCH IN THE POLITICS OF POPULA-TION, Lexington, Mass.: D.C. Heath and Co. (forthcoming).

21. Nash, op. cit.
22. Ibid.
23. Ibid.
24. Ibid.
25. Ibid.
26. The nature of this group and its objectives are covered in Chapter 4.

Index

Abortion, 27
Act to Establish a Commission on Population Growth and the American Future, 52
See also Government
African Population Conference, 20
Agency for International Development (AID), 39, 50, 55-6, 60, 79, 94, 97
Population advisory group, 51
American Population Coalition, 87
Antinatilist, 36

Berlson, Bernard, 33-6
criteria, 34, 92
BEYOND CONTRACEPTION, 14
"Beyond Family Planning", 33
criticism of, 35
Biomedical fields, 38, 59
Birth control, 30, 70
Birth rates, 11
Blacks, 20-1, 47, 60, 66, 72, 83-5, 91, 97, 98
Blake, Judith, 62
Bureau of the Census, 55

Campbell, Arthur, 92
Chasten, Edgar, 13
China, 24, 35
CLOSING CIRCLE, THE, 16
Commission on Population Growth and the American Future. 15, 21, 26, 30-1, 52, 83, 94-5
charter, 83
major theme, 27
maldistribution of urban population, 30-1
position of, 28, 93
priorities of, 30
Committee on Population of the National Academy of Sciences, 36-8, 51, 55
Davis' position, 38
Commoner, Barry, 14, 16-7, 23, 29, 62, 72
Congress, *See* Government
Contraceptive technology, 12, 30, 89
methods, 12
research, 45
Cornley, Dr. Paul, 61, 90, 93
Corporate structure, the 77-85
Cuba, 24, 34

Daly, Herman, 19
Davis, Kingsley, 24, 36-9, 62
Davis, Dr. Lawrence, 61
Death rates, 11

Decision makers, 2
Decision, 5 *See also* non-decision
Demographers 85, 94
Draper Committee, 50, 79, 80
See also Government
Draper, General William H., 50-1
Duffy, Benedict, 90

Ecologists, 24, 29, 62
Ecology: measures, 18
problems, 28
Effects of inflationary expectations, 2
Eisenhower, President, 50
Environment economics, 90
Environmental issues, 15
Erlich, Ann and Paul, 14-6, 23, 25-6, 29-30, 49, 62

Family planning, 30, 83, 88-9, 90-1, 94, 96
dialogue. 27
funding, 58
organizations, 12
"Family Planning Perspectives," 49
See also Planned Parenthood Federation
Family Planning and Population Services Act 13, 52, 83
Fertility: manipulation, 88
performance, 38
planning, 94
preferences, 90
rates, 91
research, 50
strategy, 93
Flash, William, 90
Flemister, Carl, 72
Ford Foundation, 51, 55-6, 58-9, 60, 62, 79
Freedom of choice, 28
Freyman, Moye, 92
Funding, 56-7
biases, 58-60
biomedical 58
family planning 58
pattern 57

Global framework, 14-7
Government: advisory board, 97
AID 39, 50-1, 55-6, 60, 79, 87, 94, 97
Center for Population Research (CPR - NICHD) 51, 80
commitment 49-52
congressional activity, 52, 60, 96
congressional hearings, 98

About the Authors

Elihu Bergman is Assistant Director of the Harvard Center for Population Studies. His professional specialization has been the management of development programs in the U.S. and overseas. He has worked with The Ford Foundation, VISTA, Development and Resources Corporation, and the Agency for International Development. Dr. Bergman received his Ph.D. in Political Science from the University of North Carolina where his major interest was in the political analysis of population policy.

He has contributed chapters on the American population policy process to two of the volumes in the D.C. Heath series edited by Clinton and Godwin: *Research in the Politics of Population*, and *Population and Politics: New Directions for Political Science Research*. Dr. Bergman was an organizer and served as Executive Secretary of the International Population Policy Consortium.

Peter Bachrach, professor of political science at Temple University in Philadelphia, received his Ph.D. from Harvard in 1951. His major research interests are political theory and public policy. Among his many scholarly publications two of the most recent are *The Theory of Democratic Elitism: A Critique* (Little, Brown, 1967), and, with Morton B. Baratz, *Power and Poverty: Theory and Practice* (Oxford University Press, 1970).

Professor Bachrach was a contributor to R.L. Clinton, W.S. Flash and R.K. Godwin (ed.) *Political Science in Population Studies* (D.C. Heath, 1972.)